Endorsements

"Being one of the highest paid copywriters on the planet, I went into this book thinking it'd be a good review session . . . I was wrong. Jim put together a chest of gold that has all the foundational principals you actually need, plus real and tangible action steps to cash-in immediately—no matter what your skill level. I'm upset that Jim didn't write this a decade ago. Absolute gold!!"

—Dana Derricks, Author of *Dream 100 Book*,
Dream100Book.com

"One of the greatest leveraged skills you can learn and apply is good copywriting . . . it gives you the ability to sell without being in-person and multiply your perfect sales person 24/7. I tell nearly any entrepreneur, it's worth investing in the ability of creating words that sell. Here's a perfect primer and guidebook to give you an unfair advantage."

—Yanik Silver, creator InstantSalesLetters.com and
author of *Evolved Enterprise*

Jim Edwards has done it again! Copywriting Secrets is a must have for anyone who wants to hit the nail on the head with your copywriting. Regardless of skill level, this book will help you to fine tune your copy. From the first page to the last, the book is chock full of great information. With decades of experience, Jim knows what gets people to pull out their wallets and buy. Do yourself a favor, get your copy today. You will be glad you did.

—Kathleen Gage, Business Strategist, Author, and
Speaker, www.PowerUpForProfits.com

Wow! No matter where you are in learning copywriting, whether you think you're a pro or you've never written a word to sell anything ever, this book is chock full of juicy tidbits, tips, techniques, and strategies that will help you improve your copy across the board. This is one of those books that will be pulled off my reference shelf every time I sit down to write sales copy when it really matters. Jim Edwards is a master—don't let his humble attitude fool you. Get this book, read every page, do what Jim teaches you, and enjoy the fruits of your labors as your success explodes.

—Felicia J. Slattery, Best-Selling Author of *Kill the Elevator Speech*, Co-Creator of Signature Speech Wizard, Speaker, and Business Consultant

Copywriting Secrets

How Everyone Can Use the Power of Words
to Get More Clicks, Sales, and Profits . . .
No Matter What You Sell or Who You Sell It To!

Copywriting Secrets

*How Everyone Can Use the Power of Words
to Get More Clicks, Sales, and Profits . . .
No Matter What You Sell or Who You Sell It To!*

Jim Edwards

**Foreword by
Russell Brunson**

Guaranteed Response Marketing, LLC
P.O. Box 547
Port Haywood, VA 23138

www.CopywritingSecrets.com

Printed in the United States of America

First Printing, 2018

Published by Author Academy Elite
P.O. Box 43, Powell, OH 43035

www.AuthorAcademyElite.com

Paperback ISBN: 978-1-64085-462-8
Hardcover ISBN: 978-1-64085-463-5

Library of Congress Control Number: 2018959143

Dedication

For Mom, Dad, and Patticraft, my first and best teachers in person-to-person sales, one frame at a time.

For my wife Terri, who always believed in my sales abilities even when the whole world seemed not to care.

For Buck Daniels, my first "professor" in the sales school of life.

For Russell Brunson, who showed me that people buy you as much as they buy your product.

"You are one sales letter away from being rich."
Gary Halbert

"If you can't explain it simply, you don't understand it well enough." Albert Einstein

Table of Contents

Foreword

It was almost 15 years ago when, as a newly married college athlete, I first got the itch to start my own company. I didn't know anything, except that I wanted to make some money. As I began studying, I started to discover all of the things that were essential to success.

Creating a great product, building a funnel, driving traffic, building a list and . . . writing copy.

As I learned about each of these aspects of growing an online company, I got excited about all of them, except writing copy.

I didn't enjoy writing in college, and honestly, I wasn't very good at it either.

So, despite what people told me, I focused on EVERYTHING except the copy.

I would create a new product that was much better than my competitors, yet I was confused when they would consistently outsell me.

I had a better product. Why weren't people buying MINE instead of THEIRS?

As idea after idea flopped, I started to realize that it wasn't the product that made a company successful. It was that company's ability to create a strong enough desire for that product that the customer would do anything to buy it.

AKA Sales Copywriting.

That was the key.

Eventually, I gave in and started to study good copy.

I wanted— I NEEDED— to understand the psychology behind why people buy.

The more I studied, the more I started to notice the patterns that existed in all successful marketing campaigns, and learned how to model them for the things I was selling.

As I made the shift and started to master copywriting, I noticed something very interesting . . .

Creating a great product didn't make me rich.

Building an amazing funnel didn't make me rich.

Driving traffic didn't make me rich.

Building a list didn't make me rich.

Until I learned how to write good copy, none of those things mattered because the products I tried to sell didn't sell. The traffic I tried to drive didn't convert. The funnels I built didn't persuade people to buy what I was selling.

Copywriting is what made me rich.

It is the great amplifier.

It has more impact on how much money you make with your company than anything else.

Jim Edwards became a partner of mine a few years ago when he looked at the mission we had with ClickFunnels: to help free all entrepreneurs. He called me one day and asked, "Do you want to know how you can make ALL of your customers MORE successful?"

I asked him how and he responded, "You need to help them write better copy. When their copy improves, they will sell more stuff through their funnels, and they'll stay with ClickFunnels forever."

With that as an idea, he created a powerful tool for our community called *Funnel Scripts* that has helped thousands of entrepreneurs to write copy at the push of a button . . . even if they have NO IDEA what they are doing. I've watched as this tool has helped people who have NEVER had success online to finally generate leads, make money, and find success.

When he started on this book last year, he told me that his goal was to help more people to master copywriting. That was a mighty tall order, but if anyone could, I knew Jim would.

In the right hands, this book will help you to make more money, serve more people, and increase your impact so you can change the world in your own way.

Few people on earth have studied and applied copy in more situations, for more people, and in more businesses than Jim has. This book will teach you a skill that will pay you for the rest of your life.

Don't do what I did and wait to master the art of putting words on paper and on screen to persuade people to buy from you. Throw yourself in 100%, because it's the most important skill you can learn during this life.

Russell Brunson
Co-Founder, ClickFunnels™ and Funnel Scripts

Introduction

*"I have always believed that writing advertisements is
the second most profitable form of writing. The first,
of course, is ransom notes."*
Philip Dusenberry

Nobody is born knowing how to sell.
I got started selling after I graduated from college. I quit or got fired from seven different jobs in the first eighteen months out of school. All those jobs revolved around commissioned sales. Initially, I was miserable trying to sell life insurance. I sold discount club memberships. I sold cell phones. I sold "trunked" radios (a precursor to cell phones). I sold weight loss.

I even tried pre-selling gravesites (which meant trying to sell grave plots door-to-door in Hampton, VA to people who weren't dead yet).

You name it; I tried selling it.

Everything culminated when I became a mortgage broker after I made a sale to a lady while working for a weight loss company. I sold her the weight loss program and she said, "You know, you'd be terrific in my business." I thought to myself, "Well, heck, I've been in every other business, so let me see what she's doing." She told me about the mortgage business and I said, "Well, okay," that's selling something people want and need. People need money when they want a mortgage. Turns out you don't have to work too hard to sell them money they need because they need that to buy a house.

I decided to give it a try and quickly learned that selling wasn't the hard part, getting in front of the people at the right time was. That's when I first got exposed to sales copywriting in the form of writing ads and scripts that I used to call people on the phone and ask them if they wanted to refinance.

That was the start of it. Later, I created a program on how to not get ripped off when you got a mortgage (because I'd seen a lot of people ripped off by mortgage brokers). I also wrote a book on how to sell your house yourself. When I put those products online in 1997, I learned about what we think of now as sales copy and sales copywriting as far as sales letters, email teasers and direct mail.

Once I decided to get good at writing sales copy, I did find some training. Somehow, I got my hands on a course by a guy named Marlon Sanders. I listened to recordings of him explaining the different parts of a sales letter. That's when it clicked with me that copywriting isn't just putting down words on paper and hoping that it works.

Copywriting is about structure and strategy.

I started reading books on the subject, including *Scientific Advertising* by Claude Hopkins. It's a short book, but it hits the highlights we need to know and remember. Though it helps to read people's books (obviously), one of the best things you can do is read any sales message that gets you to spend money. *That* is copy you should study because you've connected with it on an emotional level. We'll talk more about this later.

One thing to note: To my recollection, I have never written sales copy for anybody else, only for my products. I realized early on that nobody could sell my stuff better than I could. Also, when I first started selling online, I couldn't afford to hire somebody to write a sales letter for me, so I had to learn how to do it myself. The first website I ever launched had something like twenty pages. I had no clue what I was doing. Then I was exposed to the idea of a long-form, one-page sales letter, where people came and scrolled down a single page with a giant sales pitch.

So, I converted that 20-page website to a one-page sales letter. Now, if you printed it out, it might have been ten pages long, but it was one page on the website. Overnight, my sales went up 250%. That's when it clicked with me that, "Hey, if you want to make more money, writing good sales copy is the key!" It didn't have anything to do with getting more traffic. It had everything to do with how well I was able to make my sales pitch over the web.

Over the years, I've written sales letters that have done over three million dollars in sales; another one did two and a half million; another one did over a million and a half selling a $29 product. By the way, you've got to sell a lot of stuff at $29 a pop to make a million and a half bucks.

Here's the big thing to remember: nobody will write better copy for your stuff than you.

You want to be the one that creates your copy (or at least edits it) if at all possible because you're the one who knows how to connect with your audience.

It takes time to learn how to write copy from scratch . . . but it's worth it!

The cool thing is nobody is born a million-dollar copywriter. Nobody is born knowing the exact words to use for sales copy. But, unlike a fiction writer or even a non-fiction writer, sales copy follows patterns you can learn. You can use and adapt those proven patterns to quickly create copy that sells. It's the fastest type of writing you can learn and it's also the most profitable.

Secret #1

What Is Copywriting?

*Sales copywriting is anything intended to persuade
the right reader, viewer, or listener to take
a specific action.*
Jim Edwards

H ere's my definition of copywriting:

Sales copywriting is anything intended to persuade the right reader, viewer, or listener to take a specific action.
Jim Edwards

Take a moment to think about this. You want your reader, viewer, or listener to take a specific action.

Whether online or offline, these specific actions you want them to take include clicking a link, making an inquiry for more information, buying something, or going on to the next step in your sales process. With sales copy, you're trying to get somebody to click a buy button, fill out a form, buy something online, or through the mail. Maybe you want them to pick up the phone and dial a phone number or go to a physical location such as a store. When thinking about sales copy, this is true 99 times out of 100.

Sales copy can include anything from three-line newspaper ads to 40-page sales letters posted on the web. Thirty-minute infomercial videos, Facebook posts, Instagram posts, and anything in between can and should be considered sales copy.

If you want to get good at sales copy, you're saying you want to get good at enticing people to click links, fill out forms and spend money. By the way, that is a good thing to get good at! However, you don't want to over-complicate it. Most people see copywriting as a complicated thing that takes years to master and decades to get a handle on. They make it this big, complicated mess in their head. The bottom line is sales copy is anything you put in front of people to get them to click stuff, fill out forms and spend money.

When you think about sales copy that way, it becomes less daunting. This is not rocket science!

What makes copywriting different from regular writing?

Less than you think. Most people believe copywriting is a different way of thinking and writing. It's very distinct with specific patterns. Sometimes these people are right. Other times they're completely wrong.

From my experience, the best copywriting occurs when people don't realize it's copy because it's interesting to them. I used to read sales letters that came in the mail otherwise known as "free reports." It's funny to think that back in the day, you would request a free report. It was nothing but a 10, 20, or 30-page sales letter. Because it was on a topic that interested you, you didn't see it as sales copy. You saw it as a free report.

When people are interested, they're going to read it and not think about the fact that it's trying to sell them something. Now, what makes people pay attention? What makes people read and not think about the sales message? Your content addresses their fears. It speaks to their desires. It uses the words they use. It feels like a conversation with a friend or a trusted advisor.

I think a lot of people also believe sales copy is something that magically makes people do what they wouldn't ordinarily want to do. The reality is that people love to buy stuff.

That's why everybody has hellacious credit card bills. That's why everybody has made Amazon the number one site in the world to buy stuff. People love to buy. Like the old axiom says, "people love to buy; they hate to be sold." People buy when they feel like something will make them feel better or help them get what they want. Because it uses familiar, comfortable words. Again, sales copy is like a conversation with a friend or a trusted advisor.

Copywriting comes down to intention.

What do I want someone to do as a result of reading, watching, or listening to what I've created? With that in mind, sales copy can be a tweet. It can be an article. It could be a content video. It could be a Facebook Live video. It can be a meme. It can be anything you put in front of a targeted prospect. You put value in front of them. Then you invite them to take the next step which is to buy the stuff they want to buy anyway.

How much has the art or science of copywriting changed over the years?

The graphic below is a reprint of the 1900 sales catalog from Sears and Roebuck. It was reprinted actually in 1970. That's why it says $3.95 on it.

People have been buying stuff since people invented money. Before that, people bartered.

The way people talk has changed, maybe not for the better. Formal words people use and the way they address one another have changed. I'll make a little side comment here that I think people used to be a little bit more respect-ful of people's feelings and perspectives. Not in all cases, but people had manners. Today, if you go to the mall and listen to a bunch of teenagers hanging out in front of vari-ous stores, you will see that manners have escaped many. Enough on my little side rant there.

The way people talk has changed. They don't talk the same. People have the same amount of time as they did 200 years ago, but they have a hundred more things fight-ing for their attention like social media, regular mail, TV, radio, communication devices like text, Instant Messenger and cell phones. These things compete for a finite amount of a person's attention span. That's why, at the end of the day when you are drained, you say things like, "I'm done."

It's not that people are stupid or lazy. It's not that people have become dumber. People have more things fighting for their attention. It's important to understand this with your copy. In today's world you must use a lot more curiosity to stop people in their tracks and get them to pay attention to you. Also, there's a lot less buildup before you must get to the point.

My next-door neighbor is an old southern guy, super cool dude. He's a builder who built my house. He is old-school. When you talk with him, before you can get down to busi-ness, you have to do 20-minutes of warmup. Hey, how's the family? What's going on? Talk about the weather, talk about politics, talk about the neighborhood, talk about this, talk about that. Then at some point there's this deep breath. Then, what are we going to do here in this particular area?

That's the way people used to be. People aren't that way anymore. When it comes to copywriting, you've got to dispense with a lot of the warm-up. Instead, you grab them, get their attention with curiosity, and then drive them to the point you're trying to make.

How has copywriting stayed the same?

People are people who want to buy. You must have the attitude that if people understand the benefit of your product, service or software, they're going to buy it. It's your job as the person creating the copy to be a great communicator about why they need what you have. It's your responsibility.

People have hopes, fears and dreams. They've always had hopes, fears and dreams, and they will continue to have hopes, fears and dreams. They love things. They hate things. They have opinions. The better you understand the people in your niche market, the more money you'll make and the happier they're going to be because your can communicate better with them.

Understand your niche audience.

Let's talk about your niche. When people talk about copywriting, writing ads and targeting, they talk about their niche. But, most people talk about numbers. They speak of psychographics or demographics. Often, they forget that **people** in the niche actually **are** the niche. You need to understand the people. It's good to know the numbers and all that other stuff, but you need to understand the people, the person, the individuals in your niche. When we talk about your avatar, we will talk about your ideal person, whom I like to call FRED.

Understand these are people with hopes, dreams and worries. They are just like you. They want time off. They want to take care of their children. They worry about the future. They stress out over their credit card bills. They want to have a nice car. They want to provide a great future for their family. All these things are important to them. You need to know what's important to them because you're selling to people. You're not selling to a niche.

In copywriting, there's no prize for second place.

Your copy either works or you starve. That was kind of like a smack in the mouth. You don't make money when someone says, "Hey, great sales letter. Hey, I loved your video." It's nice to hear, but unfortunately, that doesn't spend. You make money when you're the one who gets people to click, buy and opt-in. That's it.

You don't go halfway with your copy. You don't do something just to see what happens and maybe it'll work out. No. You put forth a strong effort every single time. There are tools like Funnel Scripts that can help. There are tools like my wizards that can help you. The bottom line is you've got to be serious about this. You can't just do it half-assed. Because if you do, you're going to get a half-assed result.

Summary:

- People love to buy. Sales copy helps them buy from you!

- The words may have changed, but the intention of copywriting has not.

- Hopes, fears, dreams, and desire motivate people to buy.

- Anyone can get good at sales copy . . . you just need to practice.

Secret #2

One Man's Journey With Sales Copy

"The secret of all effective advertising is not the creation of new and tricky words and pictures, but one of putting familiar words and pictures into new relationships."
Leo Burnett

I do not consider myself a professional copywriter because I do not write copy for other people. I create professional level copy to sell my own stuff. That's the difference.

Nobody is born writing sales copy except maybe Ron Popeil, the dude who did the Pocket Fisherman, the Showtime Rotisserie, and the Inside the Egg Scrambler. His ability to create offers, write copy and invent products is unmatched. You and I were not born knowing how to write sales copy. The great news is you can learn.

In the early years, I designed flyers for my college fraternity parties. The pressure was on because if people didn't show up to the parties, I would lose my job as the social chairman along with the privileges.

When I worked for the mortgage banks, I wrote their ads. Every week my branch manager asked me to write an ad. I had to have it to her by Wednesday so she could send it over to the compliance department so it could run on the weekend. The ads were pretty good. But the bank rarely ran the ads exactly the way I did them because the compliance department hated me. I wanted to use words that weren't good to use in bank ads because they made the regulators nervous. It was one of the reasons why I stopped working for the bank.

Finally, the head of the compliance department called, "Look, we can tell when Jim's writing the ads and when somebody else is writing the ads. You might as well stop sending us Jim's ads because we're not going to run them." Because there were so many laws about what you could and could not say, these people were gun shy of anything that looked like exciting sales copy. It was an inauspicious beginning.

I started selling online in 1997 with decent results. At the time I started selling online, I was bankrupt and living in a trailer park (after some terrible business decisions). Here's the thing, you can't learn how to make great decisions until you make bad decisions, right? I wasn't setting the world on fire, but I was making money.

Then, in the fall of 2000, I realized that something had to change to get out of that trailer park where I'd been for six years. My ability to persuade people to buy from me had to improve. To do that, I had to run better ads, write more compelling copy for the web, and get seriously good at putting words on paper to encourage people to buy.

It was a conscious decision to do whatever it took. I was sitting in the tiny office in our spare bedroom. From that moment, I became a serious student of sales copy. I read all the classics I could get my hands on including *Scientific Advertising* and *My Life in Advertising*. You will find my recommended reading list in the appendix.

I started writing and testing copy everywhere I could. Some were for my products, but I also wrote some for a few real estate agents. I'd put something up, watch what happened, and often nothing would happen. When something good did happen, instead of chalking it up to luck, I studied what worked, kept doing that, stopped doing what didn't work, and never quit examining the good copy.

During the summer of 2000, I went to work for a company where I wrote a sales letter to sell a $97 CD-ROM. Here's a picture of it. As part of this project, I figured out how to create the auto-run CD and do the screen capture video which in 2000 was a huge deal. The sales letter made $100,000 for the company in three months, a big deal to the company.

I figured out how to create a six-figure sales funnel for this guy in less than ninety days. My wife and I moved out of the trailer, bought our little house and then he fired me in June of 2001. I'll never forget that Friday in June. With a new home complete with payments, no job and my fledgling ability to write sales copy, I was scared. I'll never forget what my wife said when I arrived home, "You basically have 30 days to make this work. By the way, if you could just make a third of what you made for him, we'll be fine."

This guy paid me $1,500 a month ($18,000 per year). That's where my self-worth was at this point. I was making 1,500 bucks a month, created a six-figure funnel for this guy and then he fired me. Over the next few weeks, I wrote or co-wrote three different sales letters. In the last four months of 2001, I made more money than I made the previous four years combined. We ended up paying off the little house in eighteen months.

That's the power of knowing how to write great sales copy. Sales copy changed my life and it can change your life too.

This picture shows our current home (from the back).

I love the picture of it in the winter. The reason I love this so much is that our little trailer was so cold, I would sit in that back-office bedroom with two chihuahuas on my lap to keep me warm. I would sit there and work on my computer and never give up on my dream of making all of this stuff work.

I am living proof that learning how to write good sales copy can change your life no matter where you are.

Summary:

- Nobody is born knowing how to write sales copy.

- Learning to write great copy can change your life.

- Read the classics like *Scientific Advertising*.

- Commit to developing your skills with copywriting.

Secret #3

Without A Strong Why,
People Don't Buy

People don't buy without a reason why.
Jim Edwards

This is the single most valuable secret I ever learned. In my opinion, this is the one that can change your life the fastest.

Burn this into your brain. *People don't buy without a reason why.* Say it with me, *"People don't buy without a reason why."*

There are ten reasons people buy.

Are there other reasons? Maybe. Honestly, I've only focused on the first five reasons why people buy. When I learned this, it changed my life. The lightbulb went off. My brain expanded. I knew how to frame my messages to people for why they should buy, and how to tie my product to their why. I now had pegs on which to hang *reasons* for people to buy.

Most people who create sales copy give prospects one reason to buy now. Usually, it involves saving or making money. That's it. It can be about making money for some people, but it's not all about making money for everyone. These ten reasons why people buy gave me a one, two, three, four punch and more in my copy.

Here are the ten reasons. We'll talk about how you put them into practice quickly in your copy. People will buy because they want to:

- Make money
- Save money
- Save time
- Avoid effort
- Escape mental or physical pain
- Get more comfort
- Achieve greater cleanliness or hygiene to attain better health
- Gain praise
- Feel more loved
- Increase their popularity or social status

The first five—make money, save money, save time, avoid effort, escape pain—resonated with me so well I committed them to memory. Those are the pegs people use to justify their buying. These are their why.

The key here is to tie multiple reasons to why people buy, not just one. Think about it this way: it's like tying down a tarp in a windstorm. If you tie down one corner of it, it's going to blow all over the place and not be under control. But, if you tie it in two, three, four, or five locations, suddenly it's right where you want it. You do this by asking certain types of questions about your product and getting creative with the answers.

Questions you can ask about your product.

You might think this sounds like work. However, putting in a little brain sweat now can translate into millions of dollars down the road. It's a fun exercise to do. Here are the questions:

1. What are five ways my product or service will help them make money?

2. How can I or my product or service help them save money over the next week, month, or year?

3. How much time can I save them and what else could they do with that time?

4. What is something they don't have to do anymore once they get my product or service? (This is how you figure out how it helps them avoid effort.)

5. What physical pain do I eliminate for them and what does that mean for their life and business?

6. How does my product or service eliminate mental pain or worry for them?

7. What are three ways I or my product can help them feel more comfortable?

8. How does my product or service make it easier for them to achieve greater cleanliness or hygiene?

9. How does my product or service help them feel more healthy or more alive?

10. What are three ways my product or service is going to help them be the envy of their friends and feel more loved by their family?

11. How will buying my product make them feel more popular and increase their social status?

If you take each of those questions and ask it honestly . . . anticipating an answer, you will be amazed at the results. Now, here's how to put this on steroids. Force yourself to come up with ten answers to each of those questions. Your brain immediately exploded at this thought, didn't it? I learned a problem-solving technique from a mentor of mine years ago. He said, "Take the problem you're trying to solve and write it at the top of a piece of paper. Then write solutions to fill up the entire piece of paper. Then go to the next page and fill that page up."

The easy answers come in the first third of the page. Then once you've exhausted the easy solutions, you need to dig in and start solving your problem and thinking outside the box. It's those answers that come later in the process that contain the real solution. If you answer each question even five times, you'll see answers that aren't obvious.

Once you go beyond those two, three, four easy answers to each question, you start digging in and thinking about who your target audience is, what they want and where they are in their life. That's where you're going to come up with copy bullets that once you write them, you're going to think, "Oh my gosh. That's awesome. That's going to make a huge difference."

I want to challenge you to take this list of questions and answer each of them multiple times. You'll come up with answers that will make a huge difference in your ability to sell.

How do you use this secret? How do you use this list?

You can tie these reasons to your offers, to your headlines, to your stories, to your bullets, to your content topics, to your calls to action, to everything. It's a lens through which everything gets focused. It's all based on that. Because once you understand the why or the whys, you can tie stuff to it that you wouldn't ordinarily, and your competitors don't.

Here are a few examples.

1. **Protein Shake**. How could we apply the ten reasons people buy to a protein shake? *Make money:* Drink this protein shake in the morning and you will have a fantastic amount of energy. You will do better at your job and probably get a raise.

   Save money: Our protein shake is 25% less expensive than the market leader, but it has superior ingredients.

   Save time: With our protein shake, you can have a nutritious breakfast in 30 seconds. You can spend more time with your kids before rushing out the door. This reason also ties in with *feel more love.*

   Avoid effort: You have your breakfast made in 30 seconds and it's delicious.

Escape physical or mental pain: Don't you hate feeling bloated all the time when you eat too much breakfast? Or, what about feeling like you're starving because you skipped breakfast? This shake solves that problem for you.

Get more comfort: I don't know how this would help you get more comfortable unless it helped with constipation.

Achieve greater cleanliness or hygiene and better health: When you drink this protein shake, you won't have bad breath when you show up at the office. Drinking this protein shake every morning is proven to help you lose weight and look great in your jeans.

Gain praise and feel more loved: You save time in the morning that you can spend with your family.

Be popular or increase social status: You lose weight. You look great. Think of all the new friends you're going to make.

2. **Executive coaching program**. It's easy to tie it to *making money*.

   Make money: Whatever you're teaching a person will help them do better in their job, get a promotion, or get recruited by another company.

   Save money: You could spend twice as much on consultants to help you do this, but we're going to teach you how to do it.

   Avoid effort: You don't have to figure this stuff out on your own. All you have to do is do what we tell you to do using our proven templates and you're good to go.

Escape physical or mental pain: What could an executive who's looking to do executive coaching be trying to do that would cause physical or mental pain? Spending too much time at the office and neglecting their family. Interesting how we tie mental pain to love and familial status. Where are they feeling pain mentally or physically? When they're spending too much time at the office and not able to spend time with their family and Little Timmy's starting to call the UPS guy "daddy." That would suck.

Get more comfort: Attend our executive coaching program where the top 1% of achievers enjoy all the benefits of having that corner office at a Fortune 500 company.

Attain fuller health: We're going to show you not only how to excel in your job, but also how to find balance in your life once and for all. You can manage your health and energy to be even more of a high performer.

Gain praise and feel more loved: We'll show you how to organize your time, so you are not staying at the office until ten every night. You'll be able to go home and keep little Timmy from calling the UPS guy "daddy."

3. **Dog training book.**

    Save money: I would start here. Learn how to train your dog yourself and avoid paying $50 an hour to somebody who probably isn't a certified professional.

    Avoid effort, escape pain: Avoid the issue of dealing with a dog bite either to yourself or a neighbor. Now, you could amp that up. Escape the potential pain of a lawsuit if your dog bites somebody. Don't get sued. This book will help you to train your dog correctly and control aggression. "Oh, dang, I better buy that because I don't want to lose my house because little Fluffy bit the neighbor's kid."

You can apply these reasons why to anything. Once you understand the reasons why, your job is simply to tie as many of them as you can to your product, service, software, or whatever it is. You must identify the reasons why people buy your stuff, specifically more than the obvious ones everybody else uses. You need to tie your product to as many reasons why as you can. Get creative. Get silly. Get inspired. Do something that relaxes you and let your mind run wild.

You might write down fifty or a hundred different things. If you find that one angle, that one unique why nobody else is using that makes all the difference in the world, or catches their attention, that's where understanding these ten reasons why people buy can transform your copywriting and mindset forever.

Summary:

- Commit these ten reasons why people buy to memory.

- Use as many of them as you can in your copy to "tie down" the prospect.

- Don't fall into the trap of always making it about making or saving money.

- Get creative in how you use these reasons . . . make yourself stretch!

Secret #4

Nobody Cares About You
In Your Sales Copy

*"People aren't interested in you.
They're interested in themselves."*
Dale Carnegie

P eople don't care about you; they only care about themselves.

That may sound harsh. You're probably thinking, "Oh Jim, that sounds kind of mean. My customers love me. Everybody likes me. That's not true; they do care about me."

Nope.

They don't care about you. Seriously, they don't. Think about when you buy stuff or pay money. What do you care about? Be honest. You care about getting your money's worth. You care about getting what was promised. You care about getting it when you want it. You care about it meeting your needs. You care about all the things related to the product and how it impacts you.

What don't you care about? The salesperson's kids. You don't care that they're having a bad day. You don't care about anything except whether you're going to get what you're supposed to get. I know this sounds harsh, but it's true. I'm sure there's a unicorn out there that is empathetic towards you and what's going on in your life and wants to know what's happening and how they can help you before they give you money, but they are the vast minority.

Here's a technique I've learned to help you make your copy all about them. It's a shortcut, a hack.

Look for these words in your copy:

"I, me, my, we, ours."

Why do you want to look for those words? Those words show where you're talking about yourself. These are the words your prospects don't care to hear because when you use them you're usually not telling them things that will benefit them.

Say this NOT THAT!

Just go back through your copy, look for any time you've used the words "I, me, my, we, ours," and change the perspective. Change the verbiage.

Example: "I want to tell you something here." Changed perspective: "Here's something you need to know," or, "There's something you need to know in this situation."

It sounds overly simplistic, but it's not. People don't want to hear about you. They want to hear about themselves. *They* want to be the hero of your sales message. Not you. They want to picture themselves getting the results, not you. They want the whole transaction to be about them, not about you.

And the way you do this is to convert your copy from talking about yourself to talking about them. How will they be enriched? How will they benefit? How will they receive what they want? Search through your copy. Look for "I, me, my, we, ours." Then rephrase, rewrite, and reposition to use the words "you, your, and yours" instead.

That's it. Sometimes you'll just rephrase a couple of sentences, or maybe only a half of a sentence. In other cases, you might look at this and say, "You know what? I'm talking about me here, and I'm getting off on a little bit of an ego trip that has nothing to do with them. I need to rewrite this to explain how this will benefit them. I need to show them how my breakthrough will help them to get the results they want."

It doesn't mean you never use the words "I, me, my, we, ours," but you consciously do it, making sure you're making it all about them. That's how you'll make it work.

It sounds harsh, but nobody cares about you. They only care about themselves when they're buying from you.

Summary:

- Make your sales copy all about them (your prospect).

- Go back through your copy and look for the words I, me, my, we, ours. When you find those words, change the perspective so it's all about them—not about you.

- Remember: prospects don't care about you. They care about having their needs met, their problems solved, their fears calmed, and their desires satisfied.

Secret #5

The Most Valuable Skill
You'll Ever Learn

*"Every product has a unique personality and
it is your job to find it."*
Joe Sugarman

The most valuable skill you'll ever learn is copywriting. People ask, "Is it worth learning how to write copy, or should I outsource it to somebody else?" The answer is yes. You need to do both.

However, I think Gary Halbert said it best.

". . . Which brings me to a crucial point. If you are in need of truly world-class copywriting, you're probably going to have to learn to do it yourself. You see, the few of us who really can do it, write copy that sells, are so much in demand, you can't even think about hiring us unless you're willing to spend an arm and a leg. Even then you'll still have to wait in line."

One of the greatest copywriters in history is telling you to learn how to do it yourself. Why? Because it's going to cost you an arm and a leg and you'll have to wait forever to get that copy back from the copywriter.

Why should I learn to write sales copy when I can outsource it?

We all need to get good at writing sales copy for several reasons. The first one is speed. If you need it fast, it's expensive. It's one thing to hire somebody to write a sales letter for you when they can fit it into their schedule and you get it in two to four weeks. But when you say, "Hey, I need a sales letter by next week." They respond, "Okay. Here we go. That sounds great. I'll be glad to charge you my next week prices."

The second reason is you don't want to be held hostage. Whenever somebody else is doing a critical business task for you, you are held hostage, even if they're benevolent. They have control, and there's not much you can do about it. Also, if you're not good at writing sales copy, you don't know if their copy is good or not.

The third reason you need to get good at writing sales copy is to make changes on the fly. Sometimes it takes longer to explain the corrections you need somebody to make than to do them yourself. From my experience, no matter what you get back from a professional copywriter, you'll have to make changes. Whether they are giving you their first draft, their third draft, or their fifth draft, you'll have to make changes. They don't know your business. They don't know your niche audience. They don't know your product. They don't know everything as well as you do. You're still going to have to work on it. Oh, and it will cost you more money to get somebody to rewrite something that's not working.

When you hire somebody to write copy for you, they're going to write copy for you. Is that sales copy going to work? You won't know until you run it. Whether it works or not, you have to pay them. You better know whether copy's good or not if you're going to hire somebody. We'll talk more in another chapter about how to hire somebody to write copy for you.

When it comes to good sales copy, you need to be able to create it. You need to be able to recognize it. You need to apply copywriting principles in everything you do. You can't isolate copywriting as a skill you don't need to develop, recognize or access. You will need a sales letter. You will need a video sales letter script. You will need ads. You can't say "I don't do copywriting. I'm the owner of the business. I'm the author, the creator and the manager of this whole process."

You need to create great copy because being good at sales copy helps you with content creation—speeches, webinars, Facebook Live, everything you're going to do.

The ability to create copy spills over into all these areas and helps you sell more.

Develop A Copywriting Mindset

A copywriting mindset is a dual thinking path. Let's say you're doing a Facebook live video and you're talking about the three things, or the three ways, or the big secret to this or that. Suddenly, you're getting to the end. While still talking, in the back of your mind you're thinking, "It's time for the close. Now I need to say something to invite them over here to do this. Let me give them a benefit and then let me give them an invitation statement." I know what you're thinking, "Damn, Jim, will I be able to do that?" Yes, you can! You can develop the discipline of the copywriting mindset and do it on the fly.

For instance, when teaching you about sales copy, I might close with: "Those are the three reasons why you have to get good at copy. By the way, if you want a cool shortcut to create amazing headlines, I invite you to check out Funnel Scripts at funnelscripts.com. We have a really cool 60-minute training you can watch where we teach you 3 great secrets about copy. Also, you can see a demo of this amazing, push-button tool that gives you over 50 different copywriting hacks for everything from sales letters, to headlines, to bullets, to video sales letters, to stealth closes and more. Go ahead and check it out."

That is what you need to be able to do. How do you develop this copywriting mindset?

1.   Focus on it.

2.   Practice.

3.   Pay attention to your results.

You can't think, "I don't need to know anything about sales copy because I can outsource it." That's stupid. I know it's wrong to call your customers stupid, but you probably won't have read this far and still be thinking that. I'm not calling you stupid; I'm calling the other people stupid. It's us against them, which by the way is a cool secret.

You need to be good (or at least proficient) at sales copy first, then you can choose which jobs you do and which jobs you outsource.

It's all about knowing how to apply those principles and being able to use them that makes a huge difference in your business. If you want to get good at copy, I'll tell you the best way to get good at copy fast. It's like getting good at pull-ups or getting into shape.

First, you have to commit. Second, you have to practice. Third, you have to do it every single day . . . even when you don't feel like it. It's not something you turn on and off. It is something you become. You have the copywriting mindset. That's how you do it. It's commitment, practice, and doing it every single day.

Commit to getting good at it. Then do it and practice it. Before you can be great, you have to be good. Before you can be good, you have to be bad. Before you can be bad, you have to try. You have to do something. Then you need to pay attention to and measure your results. What's working and what's not? It's just like with working out. I can tell you for the last six years every rep, every push-up, every mile down to the second how long it took me to run each one and the total number of exercises, circuits and everything else. Why? You have to be able to measure your progress and results in order to improve your results moving forward.

Next, you do what works and stop doing what doesn't. The only way you're going to know the difference is to do a bunch of it. The great thing about the web, social media, and cheap traffic, you get feedback not in weeks, not in months, not even in days. You get feedback instantly whether what you're doing is working or not. This is a fantastic opportunity to get good at copywriting just because you can get so much feedback so fast.

Study people who are doing it well. Look for mentors. These are people who teach you in print, in books, and through live coaching. It's just like working out. When I committed to getting in excellent shape, I found the best coach I could find to help me accomplish my objectives. Navy SEAL, Stew Smith, trains people to go into the special forces—Navy SEALs, Green Berets, MARSOC / Raiders, and Air Force Pararescue.

He coaches me to this day. When I started working out, I could do only one pull-up. Now I can do 33 pull-ups in a row, which somebody would tell you for a 50-year-old guy is almost impossible. It's the same thing with writing copy. You have to learn to flex those muscles. You may not be capable of writing a million-dollar sales letter yet. But, with enough practice, you can create a million-dollar sales letter faster than you think possible.

The other way to get good is to learn with your wallet. I'm not telling you to spend a ton of money on courses on how to write copy. I want you to pay attention to the copy that either makes you spend money now or in the past. Think about it. If the copy in someone else's funnel, video sales letter, or Facebook video makes you spend money, you need to dissect that. You need to learn which sales messages work on you and why.

Here's the reality. We are members of our own target market 999 times out of 1,000. Either you *are* a member of the target market you are going after, or you *were* a member of the target market you are trying to help. If the copy makes you spend money, it's good copy. You need to pay close attention to it.

How long does it take to become an expert at copywriting? It's a lifelong commitment. It doesn't just happen. You don't reach that point where you've "arrived."

I've met some copywriters who are "masters." They're egotistical and give off the aura, "Don't talk to me because I'm cool." It's a bit of a turnoff. Mastering copywriting is a never-ending process. You don't get into shape and then decide you don't need to work out for the rest of your life. Within a month of eating nothing but bonbons, beer, cake, steak, and all those other things, you could undo years of hard work.

Even though it's a process of developing and keeping that copywriting mindset, you can hack the process. Here's how: do it in stages. You don't need to master everything. But you need to do certain things in a specific order.

First Step: Become great at creating headlines.

Shameless plug: FunnelScripts.com will help you create amazing headlines in about 15 minutes. You can spend weeks and months developing your swipe files, or you can plug your content into the swipe files and wisdom of the ages when it comes to headlines using Funnel Scripts. The choice is up to you. The number one copywriting skill you must have to become an expert is to get really good at headlines. We'll spend more time on headlines in the next chapter.

Second Step: Become good at writing bullets.

Why do you need to write good headlines and bullets? Because every single piece of copy you will write will have a headline. The first words people see on a page, the first words you speak in a video sales letter, the title of your posts on Facebook, all use the principles of compelling headlines. Bullets that describe benefits or arouse curiosity create pressure in people to get them to take the action you desire.

In a Chapter 9 I'll give you the ultimate bullet formula, but we won't go over that now. When you write compelling headlines and bullets, you will jump far ahead of your competition. It's almost pathetic what an advantage you'll have.

Then you need to get really good at calls to action and explaining and framing offers. Become good at copywriting in this order. You might think you need to get good at explaining your offer first. No, you don't. If your headlines suck, nobody will pay attention to your offer (or even see it).

However, if your headline grabs people's attention, if your bullets build pressure and create curiosity in people, if your call to action is compelling, then your offer can suck, and you'll still make a lot more money than if your headlines suck and everything else is perfect. That's why I tell you to do this in stages. That's how you're going to quickly become an expert and develop that copywriting mindset.

Summary:

- Develop the copywriting mindset in all you do.

- Master your headlines first because they will make the biggest impact on your sales copy the fastest.

- Pay attention to sales copy that gets you to spend your own money. That's good copy!

- Never stop learning. Never stop observing. Never stop testing your sales copy.

Resources:

FunnelScripts.com—get free training and access to software that helps you get all of your sales letters, scripts, and webinars slides written (in under 10 minutes) without hiring an expensive copywriter!

Secret #6

The #1 Single Most Important Piece of Sales Copy Ever!

"On the average, five times as many people read the headlines as read the body copy."
David Ogilvy

The number one copywriting skill everybody needs is to write great headlines. I've seen statistics that eight out of ten people who see an advertisement or a webpage read the headline, but only two out of ten read the rest of the copy.

I don't know if that's accurate or not, but I can tell you from personal experience that a great headline and mediocre copy will outperform excellent copy with a weak headline. The reason is that great headlines get you up to bat more often.

If your headline sucks, nobody reads your sales letter, nobody reads your ad, and nobody watches your video. But, if you have a great headline that grabs someone's attention, people read your sales letter, read your ad and watch your video.

The purpose of a headline is simple: to get people to stop what they're doing and to start reading (or watching) whatever it is you put in front of them.

Whether it's a physical sales letter, a sales letter on the web, a video sales letter, an ad, a Facebook post, whatever it is, the headline will determine your success without exception.

Bottom Line: you have to write great headlines. That's the number one skill everybody needs to develop, no matter what you sell or who you sell it to.

The secret of a great headline is one that connects emotionally with the person who represents your perfect prospect. A well-written headline targets people emotionally, usually around either a fear or a desire. You headline targets either something they're scared of or something they really want . . . and it does so on an emotional level.

A great headline targets your ideal audience. You don't want people who aren't in your target audience reading past the headline. And, when you think about online advertising where you have to pay money for people to read your ad or click your ad, a great headline can actually cut down on the *numbe*r of clicks that you get, but massively increase the *quality* of the clicks you get.

The reason headlines are so important is because the whole sales process cannot start unless the headline stops them in their tracks and gets them to pay attention to what you're saying.

Here are the consequences of not writing good headlines.

1. You get terrible results.

2. You get frustrated and probably give up.

3. You waste a lot of time, energy, and effort in writing sales copy and sales messages that nobody reads.

4. You are always at a disadvantage because enough of the right people never see your sales message.

Let me tell you a quick story that illustrates this secret about headlines in action. Hopefully, it brings this lesson home to you.

I had been selling online for about nine years at the time. I don't remember the exact date, but I created a product called "5 Steps To Getting Anything You Want."

Let me fill you in on a little backstory.

I was bankrupt and lived in a trailer park for seven years, but turned my act around, in large part to my ability to write sales copy and sell educational products (as well as overcome some self-esteem issues). I took all the things I learned and turned it into this course I was extremely proud of. I poured tons of time, effort, research, and work into it. I recorded it as an audio CD (which was very difficult at the time), and we spent all this money to produce the product. I was utterly wrapped up in this product emotionally and financially when we started trying to sell it.

I ran ads for the product, sent email campaigns, and was excited because I had this great message to share with people. I started seeing the traffic come in but no sales. None. Zilch. Hundreds, then thousands of people visited the website, but nobody bought. I freaked out. I thought, "What the hell am I going to do?"

Then I took a deep breath and asked myself a question, "Okay, what would a good copywriter do?" And this little voice responded immediately, "They would test the head-line." So I changed the headline, and within a few minutes I had a sale. I changed it again and I had five sales. Now, I like to tell everybody, the change in that headline gave me a 500% increase in sales, but that's not true.

I had an *infinite increase in sales because* I went from zero to one sale and then to five sales with the same traffic and the same exact group of people coming through. The only thing I changed was the headline.

The original headline I ran (I'm going to paraphrase because I don't remember it exactly) was *"How I Took Myself From Bankrupt Trailer Trash To Successful Online."* The final headline I changed to was *"How To Gain A Positively Unfair Advantage In Business And In Life!"* When those sales started coming in after changing only the headline, the importance of the headline came home to me in a very real way. That first headline focused on me. Honestly, I think the whole bankrupt trailer trash idea was a turnoff. People couldn't connect with it. But with the emotional benefit of *How To Gain An Unfair Advantage In Business And In Life*, people thought, "Yeah, I'd like an unfair advantage." It's almost a guilty-pleasure-type thing, a payoff where they can fill in the blanks for what an unfair advantage meant for them individually.

Just by changing the headline I saved an entire project (and skyrocketed my business). By the way, we did six figures with that product over the next seven days. This story is the one that sticks out to me because it showed how just changing one headline saved an entire business.

How can you apply this in your situation or business to get faster results?

Acknowledge that you need to use headlines.

That's the number one thing. Most people forget or neglect the headline. Even if it's not a formal headline like you would have on a sales letter, you need to think about the titles of your videos, blog posts, etc., the same way you would think about a headline. They are that important. Same thing goes for the simplest Facebook post. Anything you're doing, you've got to have that mechanism to grab people's attention, stop them in their tracks, and make them pay attention. The headline is how you do it.

There are some shortcuts you can use to implement this immediately. One of the cool things about headlines (and almost all sales copy) is that headlines follow formulas which you can model. And, the great news is you can develop your own formulas by developing what we call a *swipe file*.

A *swipe file* is a collection of advertisements you like, and you say, "Okay, wow, that's a cool headline I could use." I found one of my most successful headlines from the cover of a video game magazine. The title on the front of *Xbox: The Official Magazine* was "The Grand Theft Auto 4 Secrets You're Not Supposed To Know." I took that and turned it into "The Ebook Marketing Secrets You're Not Supposed To Know." I used that headline, along with a $49 product, to create a six-figure business.

A *swipe file* is just a collection of ads that grab your attention. I like to pick up the "Bottom Line" reports, People Magazine, the National Inquirer, direct mail, catalogs, and more. And, most importantly, any advertising that makes you buy (spend your own money) is something to put into your *swipe file*.

Here are some headline templates you can use immediately.

The first group is "how to" headlines, so it's how to get results. Remember, people are avoiding pain; they're seeking pleasure.

How To Get _____

- *How To Get A Better Score On Your Next PT Test*
- *How To Get Rid Of Acne*

Another thing that you can do is take a little riff on that how-to headline by giving people a timeframe.

How To _____ In As Little As _____

- *How To Double Your Pushups In As Little As 10 Days*

- *How To Get Rid of Acne In As Little As 24 Hours*

It's whatever appealing result they want—for how to do something or get something—in a timeframe that they go, "Oh yeah, that'd be cool!" Be careful that the timeframe is believable. Then you can take it even further.

How To _____ In As Little As _____ . . . even if you _____!

This headline template is where you take away a thing they think is stopping them, an objection they might have, or a barrier they see in the way.

- *How To Pass Your PT Test In As Little As 2 Weeks . . . even if you can't do a single pull-up right now!*

- *How To Get Rid Of Your Pimples In As Little As 7 Days . . . even if you've tried everything else and failed!*

That ending is a great one to use by the way. You can use that for anything . . . *even if you've tried everything else and failed.*

Here's one more "how to" headline template that works really well.

How Every _____ Can _____

- *How Every New Military Recruit Can Become A PT God In 12 Weeks!*

- *How Every Teenager With Pimples Can Have Clearer Skin Fast!*

The second group of headline templates you can use is what I call "ways to get what you want." It works well with numbers too. The key here is to use an odd number like 3,5,7,9—they seem to work better and carry more credibility. These headlines work great for articles, blog posts, and videos because they arouse curiosity. People want to read to find out all the different ways or options for getting a result.

5 Quick And Easy Ways To _____

- *5 Quick And Easy Ways To Max Out Your Pushups*

- *5 Quick And Easy Ways To Get Rid Of Pimples*

3 Fast Ways To Get _____ And Avoid _____

- 3 Fast Ways To Get A Better PT Test Score And Avoid "Fat Boy" PT Squad

- 3 Fast Ways To Get Rid Of Acne And Avoid Embarrassment

Then we can ramp them up with an "even if" statement which lets them off the hook for past failure (something everyone wants)!

5 Quick And Easy Ways To Get _____ . . . Even If _____!

- *5 Quick And Easy Ways To Get A Higher PT Test Score . . . Even If You Failed Your Last Test!*

- *5 Quick And Easy Ways To Get Rid Of Pimples . . . Even If Your Social Life Is A Disaster Right Now!*

Again, you want to acknowledge something they're worried about and tell them it's going to be okay.

The third group of headline templates that work well and grab people's attention revolves around "mistakes." People are petrified of making mistakes. In school, we learn that mistakes are BAD. Think about that for a minute. A test score in school penalizes you for making mistakes. No wonder people get so freaked out! Use this to your advantage with mistakes headlines that grab attention.

Which Of These _____ Mistakes Will You Make?

- *Which Of These PT Testing Mistakes Will You Make?*

- *Which Of These Pimple Treatment Mistakes Will You Make?*

Then you can throw in who they are in the group to connect with their identity and grab their attention.

_____ Mistakes All _____ Need To Avoid!

- *PT Test Training Mistakes All New Recruits Need To Avoid!*

- *Acne Treatment Mistakes All Pregnant Women Need To Avoid!*

_____ Mistakes Every _____ Needs To Avoid!

- *3 PT Testing Mistakes Every Marine Needs To Avoid!*

- *5 Acne Treatment Mistakes Every Teenager Needs To Avoid!*

The fourth template we can use is "warning" headlines. I don't remember where I read this, but it was life-changing to understand. It's a little-known fact about how animals respond to danger, especially in the jungle. When one species of animal sounds a warning call, whatever it is, ALL animals respond and pay attention. But when the all clear sounds, it has to be specific to that type of animal. If a Macaw starts screaming that a tiger is about to attack, all the animals pay attention. But when the Macaw calls the all clear, the only ones that pay attention are the Macaws.

Using a warning headline is a way to get everybody's attention, even if they're not in your direct target audience. You have to be careful not to abuse it or have it turn out to be a bunch of hype because that'll make people mad. People are trained to pay attention to warnings. Warning labels appear on virtually everything in our lives from prescription medication to plastic bags on plush toys. People respond to being scared, so grab their attention with a warning headline!

WARNING: you can overdo this

Don't be like the little boy who cried wolf. If you use a warning headline, do it intelligently and realistically. Otherwise, you kill your credibility.

WARNING: Here's What Every _____ Needs To Know About _____

- *WARNING: Here's What Every New Recruit Needs To Know About PT Testing In Bootcamp*

- *WARNING: Here's What Every Teenager Needs To Know About Over-The-Counter Acne Treatments*

WARNING: Don't Even Think About Trying To _____ Until You Read This

- *WARNING: Don't Even Think About Trying To Pass Your Next PT Test Until You Read This*

- *WARNING: Don't Even Think About Trying To Get Rid Of Pimples Until You Read This*

Here are some other headline templates you can try that work extremely well under a variety of circumstances.

Here's The Perfect Solution If You Want _____

- *Here's The Perfect Solution If You Want To MAX Your Next PT Test*

- *Here's The Perfect Solution If You Want Clearer Skin This Week*

Here's The Perfect Solution If You Want _____ (even if _____)

- *Here's The Perfect Solution If You Want To Be A PT God (even if you can barely do 20 pushups right now)*

- *Here's The Perfect Solution If You Want Clearer Skin (even if you feel like there's no hope)*

My Proven _____ Method To _____

- *My Proven "Pullup Push" Method To Double Your Pullups*

- *My Proven "Clear Skin" Method To Get Rid Of Your Pimples Forever*

Once you realize headlines are templates, you'll notice them all around you. A great place to look is in line at the grocery store. Look at the headlines and bullet text on the front of the tabloid magazines. Don't read the stories about celebrities interbreeding with aliens from outer space, see the headlines about those topics, how they're structured, and how you could adapt them for your own headline needs.

Recognize that headline templates are all around you. Pay attention to them. Develop your swipe file. You'll start getting ideas, especially for everything from articles and blog posts to email teasers, by paying attention to which headlines catch *your* eye.

That's a shortcut, by the way: develop your swipe file and pay attention to formulas that help you to create headlines fast.

The most significant piece of advice I have for you when it comes to headlines, besides acknowledging the fact that you need to use them, is to consciously spend time on your headline and not treat it as an afterthought like many people do.

In many cases, I devote 50% of the time I spend creating the entire sales piece to the headline—whether it's a sales letter, an e-mail teaser, a postcard, a Facebook post, or something else. If that's going to take me two hours, I might spend an hour on the headline (not all the time, but often). You need to give it the time and attention it deserves because it's such a critical element.

The headline starts the entire sales process.

Summary:

- Spend a lot of time working on your headlines, especially for sales copy and ads. It's the #1 factor that determines success or failure.

- Never post anything online without a headline or compelling first statement. If in doubt, use curiosity to pull people in (Example: The #1 Headline Mistake People Make That Bleeds Them Dry).

- Once you have a headline that works, TEST new headlines against that one to see if you can improve results. I've seen as much as a 500% improvement in sales just by changing a single headline.

Secret #7

It's NEVER "One Size Fits All"

"I don't know how to speak to everybody,
only to somebody."
Howard Gossage

There is a mistake most people make, especially online. They don't segment their traffic, which means they give the wrong message to the wrong audience. Remember what we said about headlines? This mistake is especially common with headlines.

Today, everybody puts up a webpage. When it's done, people are so excited and think, "Oh my God, my webpage is done. Thank you, God. Now I can start selling." They direct traffic to that sales page, but the problem is that all traffic is not made up of the same people. In fact, there are three different types of traffic you need to be aware of when creating your sales copy, especially headlines.

Here's a quote from Eugene Schwartz who was a master copywriter from years past. When he wrote this statement, the internet didn't exist.

> *"If your prospect is aware of your product and has realized that it can satisfy this desire, your headline starts with the product. If he is not aware of your product but only has the desire itself, your headline starts with the desire. If he is not yet aware of what he really seeks but is concerned with the general problem, your headline starts with the problem and crystallizes it into a specific need."*

In our online world, there are hot, warm, and cold traffic sources.

- Somebody who is on your email list or follows you on social media and knows your name is a hot source.

- Someone who is looking for a solution to a problem, but they don't know about you yet is a warm source.

- Someone who doesn't even realize there's a solution out there but knows they have a problem is a cold source.

Each group needs to receive a different message from you. Therefore, it's not one-size-fits-all.

So I'll give you an example using the physical training (PT) testing example from a good friend of mine, Stew Smith. Stew is a former Navy SEAL and a graduate of the US Naval Academy who trains all the special ops guys coming out of the Naval Academy. He also prepares people for the military, police, and firefighter professions. Stew sells information about PT testing and preparation for physical training tests to either enter or stay in some physically demanding occupations. Here are the different messages he sends depending on the group.

Hot traffic source:

> People who know Stew, who are on his newsletter list, see specific copy every time he releases a new book about how to get ready for a PT test. It's straightforward. All the ads, all the copy, all the social media posts say, "Hey, Stew Smith just came out with a new book called, "How To Pass Your Next PT Test In As Little As Two Weeks. You need to check it out because it's going to show you how to do this, this, this, this, and this."

This direct message works well for those people who know Stew.

Warm traffic source:

> Stew targets people on Facebook who don't know him, but are in the military or some other profession where they have to get ready for a PT test. He writes ads about preparing for the PT test, getting in shape (in case you weren't), what to do if you're failing, and how to improve in specific areas. All of these ads and posts direct people to his book, but he needs to get their at-

tention first with a solution they are already looking for. Then he leads them to the books. They know their need (get ready for a PT test), they know their desired result (pass the test), so they are receptive to ads and content around those topics.

Cold traffic source:

This group of people is in terrible shape. They consistently fail their PT tests, and they don't know what to do to fix the problem. Therefore, they get messages around topics like "Failed your last PT test? Don't know what to do? You're not alone! Here's a solution."

With the targeted approach, each group gets different language in their sales message.

However, most people's sales copy reads, "We help people pass their PT test!"

What's wrong with this sales copy? People who already know you don't need that information. They need specifics about how you can help them now.

People who don't know you, but are looking for a solution, *may* respond to that general message. They will respond better to specific messages like "We help people pass the FBI academy PT test;" or "We help people pass the RASP selection PT test;" or "We help people get ready for a SEAL contract."

Finally, for people who don't even know there's a possibility they could pass their PT test or they're focused on a specific problem like being overweight, struggling with slow run times, or recovering from overuse injuries, that general message won't resonate with them at all.

When writing sales copy, you need to be conscious of these three groups. Depending on where you are in your business, you may have a lot of people in one group vs. another. If you're just getting started, the majority of the people will be in the warm and the cold groups. If you have a business, product, or a service that requires a lot of explanation or people don't know the solution exists, then most of your traffic is going to be cold.

If your traffic is cold, your message needs to focus on people's problems. Then you transition from talking about the problem to the need followed by your solution to that need. Just like with headlines, it's crucial to attract the right people. Getting the correct sales message to the right group of people can make a huge difference in whether or not you lose money, break even, or you're profitable.

By the way, the easiest place to segment your traffic using this approach is on Facebook. And, fortunately now with tools like *ClickFunnels*, it's a lot easier to set up several different landing pages to steer each type of traffic to, so that you can put the right message in front of the right people.

Segmenting your message makes all the difference when someone is looking at your headline and your ad. That person quickly decides, "Is this for me? Does this guy understand my problem or not?"

So, what are the consequences of not applying this particular secret?

You'll have bad conversions because you're putting the wrong message in front of the wrong people. I'll give you a little hypothetical story to illustrate this.

You are having a conversation with somebody about Uncle Jim's anti-virus software you sell. This person knows they have a virus, but they have no clue what to do about it. In this case, your message should focus on you and your product.

But what if you don't do that? What if you ignore them and tell them only what you want to say to them?

The person says to you, "I think I've got a virus on my computer and I don't know what to do about it."

You respond with information about Uncle Jim's anti-virus software, how it got a five-star review from the International Board of Software Reviewers and they look at you and say, "Well, how do I get this virus off my computer?"

You say, "Uncle Jim's anti-virus software is ranked number one in the world."

This conversation doesn't make any sense! You're talking about your product and yourself, and they're talking about their problem.

Now, you might say to yourself, "Honestly, Jim! Surely, they can make that mental leap to 'Hey, it's the number one anti-virus software in the world. Obviously, it'll take the virus off my computer.'"

But will it? Is it the right software for *their* computer and the virus that's affecting *them* right now? They don't know the answer, and you're not giving it to them. Your software is *not* their focus! Your brand is *not* their focus! Your name is *not* their focus! You've got to get in sync with the conversation they want to have *first*, so you can steer them towards the solution you're selling.

So if they're focused on problems, you start the conversation with the problem to get in sync with them. Then show them you've got the solution.

If your new friend with the infection is looking for a specific result or solution such as, "Hey, I need antivirus software," but they're not saying, "I need Uncle Jim's anti-virus software." Then you lead with, "Oh, you need anti-virus software? Check this out!"

But if that same person says, "Hey, I'm thinking about Uncle Jim's anti-virus software," then they need to see a message about Uncle Jim's anti-virus software specifically, *not* a general ad about anti-virus software. If they say, "I have a problem with my computer running slowly, and it shuts off without warning sometimes." You *don't* say, "You have a virus!" You say, "Oh, your computer is running slow and shutting down unexpectedly? There are three typical reasons for that. Let me tell you what they are." Then you lead them to potential fixes, including anti-virus software.

Now I know the last point is a fine line (and you may need to re-read it), but the fine line is the difference between selling 1% of the people who show up to your website, and selling 20% of the people who show up at your website!

Shortcut: The fastest way to figure this out is to think through the conversations you could have with hot, warm, and cold people about your product or service.

- What would be the conversation with someone who knows who we are and what we do?

- What would the conversation be like with someone who is aware they have a problem, but they're not aware of us?

- What would the conversation be like with people who know they have a problem, but they have no clue a solution even exists?

To put this into action on a website quickly, make three different copies of the webpage to create three different landing pages. Then, change the headline of each page to match the traffic temperature based on the traffic source (hot, warm, cold). Then look at the sales copy from your audience's standpoint and adjust the existing text to fit. A lot of times you can get 99-yards down the field with a few simple tweaks, especially at the very beginning of your sales message (often called the "lead").

For the sake of expediency, don't try to target each group at the same time. Pick the one you think you can get the most mileage from the fastest and concentrate on them first.

For example, if you have an email list, focus all your marketing on this hot traffic source first! Do the same thing with your followers on Facebook and other social media. After that, target the warm market, and then finally write copy for the cold market. By the way, the cold market is usually the largest. If you can connect with them, that's how you break into the world of *big* sales!

Summary:

- Acknowledge the different audiences who can use your product or service.

- Identify those audiences and commit to putting the right messages in front of them.

- Don't be lazy and fall into the trap of one-size-fits-all with your sales messages.

Secret #8

Meet F.R.E.D. (Your Ideal Customer)

"Mirror the reader to himself and then show him afterward how your product fits his needs."
Raymond Rubicam

Copywriting does not happen in a vacuum. When you are writing copy, you are writing to a specific group of people. More specifically, you are writing text that could be viewed by a million different people, but it gets read one person at a time. It's important you know who you're writing to. You've most likely heard the term "avatar" which refers to the perfect representation of your ideal customer. I call your avatar Fred, your new best friend.

In this secret, we will talk about how to define your target audience avatar in a way you can use in the real world, why defining your target audience matters, easy tools to allow you to quickly identify your avatar, and how to look at your avatar differently.

I will teach you the 20% that's going to give you 80% of the results. You will be super-efficient with your energy, focus and effort. Many times when people talk about avatars, they either make it complicated, or they only teach you to create a story about your avatar. While this is useful information (and better than not having one), you need to define your avatar in a way that helps you create fantastic copy.

Why do you need to define your Fred?

You need to know the words he uses and how he expresses his ideas. You need to know what's on his mind and what's going on inside Fred's head. Because what's going on inside his head will determine whether you sell something or not, whether you get an opt-in or not, whether you get a click or not.

You need to know what's going on in Fred's mind better than he does. You need to know how to enter the *conversation* going on inside his head. If you aren't talking about what he wants to talk about, if you don't show him what he wants to see, if you don't tell him what he wants to hear, he will ignore everything you have to say.

How to define your target audience?

Before we go any further, you need to know that I got thrown out of business school. I got a D-minus in Statistics. The only reason I passed was because I agreed to drop out of business school and major in History. Everything I'm teaching you comes from my direct experience; it is not theory. This information is all based on hands-on, in the trenches, selling people stuff, belly-to-belly, or through the web.

First, figure out who they are. There are two schools of thought when it comes to defining your target audience. I prefer the term "niche" instead of target audience because niche refers to a specific group or sub-group of people.

Many times, when you hear people talking about niches, they're talking about keyword counts or keyword numbers. "My niche has 100,000 searches for this," or "My niche has a million whatevers." Here's something you need to understand. People will buy from you. A keyword count doesn't buy from you. More specifically, people will buy from you one person at a time. You have to know who these people are and what they have in common that makes them belong to the group.

When it comes to defining your niche, there are two schools of thought. One is demographics. You measure and look at things like age (43-year-old white male). You look at gender. You look at the location. Demographics are numbers-based.

The problem is that demographics are broad. Though I can tell you that the typical people who buy from me are between the ages of 40 and 65, 60% are women, 40% are men, and they live in the United States, Australia, Great Britain, Canada, and then smatterings all around the world, that's still too broad to be able to sell anything. It's interesting that people will key in on demographics, but if you try and use demographics exclusively, you're going to have a tough time selling anything to anyone.

I prefer using psychographics. Psychographics refers to what's going on inside of a person's head. What are they thinking? What's motivating them? What are their attitudes or aspirations? I use psychographics first, and then I refine my niche with demographics.

Psychographics are things I understand. Fred has specific problems. Fred also has interests, desires and goals. These are the things that matter in sales copy. If I know your problems, if I understand your interests, if I know your desires, if I know your goals, then I know how to communicate with you. I know how to put little presents out in front of you that get your attention. I know how to get in touch with your feelings. I know how to understand and identify various situations you're going to find yourself in where I can put my sales message in front of you.

You can use this information to narrow down your message because understanding your audience is more about excluding people than it is including people. I would rather have an audience of 10,000 laser-focused people who I can give specific sales messages to, as opposed to 100,000 people who are casually interested in something that I'm going to waste a ton of money putting sales copy in front of that will never buy anything.

You need to define who your target audience is and you need a specific way to do that. That's exactly what I'm going to help you with right now.

There are really three levels of definition.

The first is the idea of a niche. A niche is very broad. An example is real estate. Real estate is too general to be able to run ads and write meaningful sales copy.

Secondly, we need to move into what I like to call a sub-niche. This is a narrower part of the bigger niche. In our example, a sub-niche would be a real estate investor. Within this sub-niche there are different types of real estate investors. I personally have been in several different niches. I've been a flipper. I've been a buy and hold. I've been a hard-money lender.

Finally, we need to drill down even more to find our Fred. Now we look at a micro-niche where we get laser-focused. Again, as the sub-niche was a smaller part of the broad niche, a micro-niche is a narrower part of a sub-niche. In this case, we might talk about flippers—someone who buys a house, and turns it around in 30 to 60 days, hopefully, at a profit.

Now this micro-niche person is Fred . . . Fred the Flipper. Fred the Flipper has very different needs than Ronnie real estate agent or Randy real estate investor, or Sue and Johnny home buyer. Understanding Fred, the Flipper helps your sales copy take a massive leap forward because you have a better understanding of who they are.

Why do you want to narrow the field like this? First, it's easier to target. When targeting things like your ads on Facebook or Google AdWords, buying media from other websites, buying ads on sites or in people's newsletters, you've got to know who you want to show your ads to.

It's also easier to find your niche because you know what they look like. You can find more people and eliminate those who don't match your perfect target. You're not only going to make more money, but you're also going to save money on ad costs.

Narrowing down makes it easy to communicate because you use the words they use. Sales copy uses the magic words to convert them. These are the words they're using right now, so they know you hear them, understand them and you're not talking down to them. The right message is the message that contains the words they're using, they want to hear and targets them directly.

Narrow is better.

Despite what some will tell you, it is tough to put out a message that is going to be effective with a million people. That's more of an institutional, large-scale, general-type of offer. If you're making a general-type offer, and can find a group of a million that makes sense, and do well with your ads, then do it. Most of us do much better if we can go a few feet wide and a mile deep rather than going three feet deep and a mile wide.

How are we going to define our avatar?

I like to call my avatar Fred. Fred started as an acronym for Fears, Results, Expectations, and Desires (F.R.E.D.). That's where the name came from, but after diving into this and using this for years, I figured out a better way to explain or to codify what an avatar is.

You need to give your avatar a name because when you sit down to either write copy from scratch or use a tool like Funnel Scripts, you need to have a specific person in mind. Remember, I said that you might sell to a million people, but they each buy one at a time. You need to communicate to a specific person instead of to a group.

In this example we used above, our house flipper's name is Fred The Flipper. If your niche is gardeners, are they green thumbs? I have a friend that sells workout stuff. He refers to his avatar as couch potatoes because they refer to themselves as couch potatoes. He helps them become reformed couch potatoes. Are they mommies? Are they sci-fi fanatics? What are they? Who are they? What is their name? You need to give them a name. You can change it later, but you need to refer to a specific person.

Another thing you can do, and I have done this, is search Google for the name. See what pictures come up under Google images. Then, pick one and print it out. When you're preparing your sales copy, you visualize talking to or writing to that specific person. It makes a huge difference in your ability to create quality copy.

Now that we know *who*, we need to talk about *what* these people want.

When I was getting started, I thought, "I need to sell people what they need. What do these people need?" What I learned was nobody buys what they need. Everybody needs to lose weight, but they don't do anything about it. People buy what they want. Pointblank. End of story. All that matters is **people buy what they want, NOT what they need**.

You need to sell people what they want. You need to *want* to sell people what they want, not what they need. Some people get heartburn over this. I'm not saying you don't include what people need in whatever you sell, but, from the standpoint of your copy, you only talk about what they want. Do not tell them what they need. Because just like telling a child they need to go to bed, they'll think, "Screw you. I want to stay up, snort pixie sticks, and watch the all-night Barney tube marathon on NetFlix." That's what they want!

Don't talk about what people need. Talk about what people want. Include what they need in whatever you sell them or whatever service you offer them. But, when you write copy, you only talk, speak, show, and include what they want. It is crucial you understand this distinction. Often, when I've taught this, people say, "Well, that's not ethical. You need to sell them what they need or they won't get the result you promised." What I'm saying is you sell them with what they want; and you include what they need.

Here's F.R.E.D. at the next level.

PQR2 is the secret code to your audience's brain. What does PQR2 stand for?

Problems
Questions
Roadblocks
Results

Picture this. Fred is at the top of a chasm on one cliff looking at another cliff across the way. Your people are here as well.

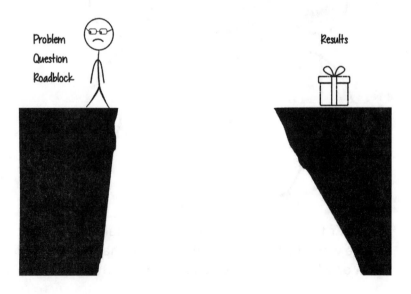

He wants to be on the other side. How is he going to bridge the gap? Your sales copy will bridge the gap. What's on this side where Fred is standing? He's aware of his problems. He's got questions. There are roadblocks. Definite things hold him back. He is completely tuned in to his problems, his questions, and his roadblocks. He's also tuned in to the results he wants, which are over there on the other cliff. He wants to go from here to there.

What's going to help him do that (this is an important distinction) is your sales copy. It is not your product, service, or software.

He can't physically make this leap until he makes it in his mind *first*. Your sales copy helps him do that. His problems, his questions, and his roadblocks have him firmly planted on the first cliff. What he wants are results which are on the other side. These PQR2s are what define your niche. You take these problems, questions, roadblocks and results and turn them into a sub-niche or micro-niche.

Let's look at it from another perspective. We know where Fred is. Fred only thinks about PQR. He wants results, but the vast majority of people are caught up in their problems. It's like he's stuck. On the first cliff, we have the stick. On the other, we have the carrot. The power of the stick is much more prevalent in his world than the carrot is. In fact, if you look at it, it's 3:1. Fred sees problems, questions and roadblocks on one side and his desired results on the other side.

To move him across the chasm, you build a bridge with your sales copy. If he has questions, you show him you have answers. If he's got roadblocks, you show him how to remove them because all he's thinking about are these problems, questions and roadblocks. For him to move forward, he's got to see you can solve problems, provide answers and remove roadblocks. Only then will he believe he can get those results. Only then is he willing make that journey across the bridge from where he is now to where he's going to be (and buy)!

Any form of sales copy can be used to help Fred move across the chasm. It could be a video sales letter, a long-form sales letter, a content video, an article, or any copy. Whether you think of it as sales copy or you think of it as content, marketing, this is what's going on inside of his head. You get in tune with the problems, questions and roadblocks. Then start knocking those down and show Fred how to get results with what you sell.

Remember when we discussed cold, warm, and hot traffic? This concept deals with cold traffic and some warm traffic. If you want to go crazy with your sales copy and make money, you have to address cold traffic. Well, this is how you do it. You understand your avatar so well that when they're in the cold stage, you're able to communicate with them through problems, questions and roadblocks.

Focus on your avatar's problems, questions, roadblocks and results. You'll have Fred's 100% attention. He can't think about anything else. The conversation going on inside his head is only about these four things: problems, questions, roadblocks and results.

The question for you, then, is how do you know what's going on inside Fred's head? Where and how do you find out the problems, the questions, the roadblocks and the results for your target avatar?

How do you discover Fred's PQR2?

1. **Live interaction.** When you're at a big event, listen to what people complain about. Where's the problem? Where are they frustrated? Where's their pain? What questions are they asking?

2. **Look at yourself.** We are often members of our target audience either currently or in the past. What are your problems? What are your questions? What are

your roadblocks? What are the results you desire? You are a great insight into what Fred is feeling, holding him back and has him up late at night in a cold sweat.

3. **Forums.** Forums are still alive and well on the world-wide web. Don't discount or ignore finding forums with specific members of your target audience. Mine these for problems, questions, roadblocks, and the results they seek.

4. **Your website's help desk.** If you don't have one, you should if you're selling anything to anyone. Your help desk is a great place to look for the problems, questions and roadblocks. I've gotten some million-dollar product ideas out of my help desk. You see trends as well as specific questions. You may notice that five people had the same issue in the last two weeks. If so, you have a new product idea.

5. **Popular products.** Look at specific things like e-books, print books, physical products, or popular products to identify problems, questions, roadblocks and results people are looking for.

6. **Answer sites like https://www.quora.com/ and Answers.yahoo.com.** Sites like these are great places to look for questions people ask, especially if you're not in the market to teach people the latest and greatest techniques for selling stuff on Instagram. For instance, my buddy Suzanne, does stuff around animal behavior. Animal behavior, questions, and problems have not changed in the last twenty years. The answers may have changed, but the customer questions have not changed for your target audience.

7. **Surveys.** I love to do surveys because you get up-to-the-minute thoughts and answers about

people's problems. These are especially helpful if your niche is continually changing.

8. **Social media sites.** You can find problems, questions, roadblocks, and results people are looking for in Facebook groups and Twitter. Look at hashtags for what's trending.

Look at these tools and sources. We've listed eight here, but there are more ways to do it as well.

How do you use these tools to find what you need?

1. **Answer sites.** Go to answers.yahoo.com and type in "real estate flipping" and hit enter. You will see the questions people are asking like: Is real estate flipping profitable? What is real estate flipping? Does real estate flipping still make sense? How do I get started at real estate flipping with no money down? How do I stay motivated? Are there people that do this internationally? How do I attract new partners? How do you start as an investment vehicle? Is it possible in another country? What's the ultimate guide? Where is the best place to learn about this? How do you locate investors?

   You become educated about the questions people who are potentially in your target niche are asking. Then, use these questions to create content, headlines, talking points, and the beginning of stories.

2. **Surveys.** You might not be interested in doing a survey yourself through a site like surveymonkey. com. The good news is you don't have to. Here's a cool thing. You can find other people's surveys

and look at the results. Just go to Google and do the keyword search plus the word "survey." Ex: flip real estate survey. You'll find data you can review to know more about what's going on with Fred.

3. **Social media.** Another way is to just ask people on Facebook a question. Personally, I think this is one of the smartest things that you can do. Ask in a group. Ask on a page. Ask on your profile page. Ask people what their hardest struggle is or what their biggest question is. People will tell you they're concerns, questions, and roadblocks. A fun way to get people to answer questions is to use a little meme as part of your post on social media to attract attention. The bottom line is that Facebook and social media are great ways to do surveys.

4. **Google search.** Search for your keyword, plus the word FAQ, mistakes, questions, or top 10. You will get a ton of information that can help you. Look at the top results to see what questions people ask.

5. **Popular products.** This is like "funnel hacking" or "audience hacking". What do you look at in an existing product? If it's a book, look at the table of contents. Look at the chapters and see what they are about. Look at the index for keywords, terms, or maybe things you never thought about. You can look at sales copy for offers on people's funnels and websites. You can also look at feedback because that will show you how the market responds. The five stars on Amazon will say, "this is awesome". Look at the one stars to see what people are bitching about. Looking at this information gives you real insight into what people want. They're looking for meat. They're looking for answers to their

questions. They're looking for value. They're looking for step-by-step information. They're looking for content.

What these come down to and what you need to focus on in your copy is what people really want. Fred is on the first cliff. He wants to be on the other one. Fred wants to change the way he feels. He wants less of some emotion and more of another. He's stuck in his head with PQR2 because of fear. He feels fear, stress, pain, or boredom. That's his reality. That's where most people are. Fred wants to change the way he feels.

But, you can't change the way he feels by focusing on money. Most business people key in on the money. Well, the money isn't it. What Fred wants is to change from fear to security. He wants to feel like things are going to be okay, and he's going to be safe. He wants to go from stress to peace. He wants to go from feeling all frazzled to, "Huh, that feels good." He wants to go from pain to comfort. He wants to go from boredom to fun.

By the way, one of the most overlooked components of any sales copy is focusing on fun. See how you can add fun. That's one of the keys that we use to sell the Jim Boat, a cruise seminar we've done since 2007. It's always on a different topic. Sometimes, on eBook marketing, other times building your newsletter. It has been a different topic each time that had different hot buttons we would key in on.

One of the important things that sells it is the fun. The fun of going on this cool big boat, and having a good time with a whole bunch of like-minded people. We always end up on some tropical island, sitting under a palm tree just visiting, drinking umbrella drinks, and having a great time with everybody!

Paint the picture for your avatar of the cool stuff they will learn as well as the fun they will have. Don't discount the fun part.

How are we going to use PQR2 with your target audience? I want to hammer it one more time. Fred is 100% tuned in to what's going on inside of his head. That's it. He is tuned in to his problems, his questions, his roadblocks, and the results he wants, but hasn't gotten yet. There's a technical term for this called your Reticular Activating System. Basically, you tune in to and recognize what you're already looking for at the exclusion of everything else.

All your content, whether it's free or paid, needs to key in on the same thing. Your ads, your blog posts, your videos, Facebook and social media posts, live videos, memes and your webinars are all based around Fred's PQR2. Your headlines focus on his problems, his questions, his roadblocks, and his results.

Your assignment

Your assignment is to assemble Fred. You need to make Fred whole. You need to get into action with your buddy, Fred.

First, define your Fred. Go from a large niche down to sub-niches then to micro-niches. You can have more than one. Think of your niche like the circles on a dart board. When you throw the dart at the board, a regular niche is the outer rim. A sub-niche is the inner rim. The micro-niche is the bullseye. You need to identify who you're going after.

Next, identify and write down Fred's top two problems. Then, what are Fred's top two questions? Then, what are his two big roadblocks?

Finally, what are the top two results that Fred desires?

Don't be like most people and skip this assignment. Medium achievers will write down two for each area, but the overachiever will come up with five to ten. I want you to create a list of five to ten for each because the first two are the easy ones. Three to four extras you come up with will make you think. The fifth one is probably the magic connection.

If you do the ten, that's when you dig in and deeply connect with Fred. You want to get to the ones in each area that have emotional kick. How are you going to use this insight about Fred? Use it just like magic.

Let me show you some headlines you can base on Fred's PQR2.

- You Don't Have To Be A Pro Real Estate Flipper To Have Fun Doing Deals, Guaranteed.

- New, The Secret To Automatically Finding Great Deals Fast, Guaranteed.

- Discover The New Way To Find Great Deals Fast.

- How To Find Great Deals Fast, So You Can Avoid Buying A Poison House That Destroys Your Business!

- At Last! The Real Secret To Finding Great Flips Fast Is Revealed.

- How To Find Great Deals In As Little As One Week, Even If You Have No Money Of Your Own To Invest!

All I did was take Fred the Flipper's problems, questions, roadblocks, and results put them into those headline templates we discussed in Secret #6. Instantly, we've gone from, "How are we going to use this research?" to "Holy crap! We're writing copy and it's good."

Let's do some **email subject lines** based on Fred's PQR2s.

- Real estate investing hack.

- Find great deals, two great ideas.

- The real secret to find great deals when flipping.

- Find great deals in half the time. Two shortcuts for real estate investing.

- To find great deals, this works like crazy.

- For house flipping, this works like crazy.

- The fastest path to flipping success.

- Here's an example of what works to find great deals.

- Here's a shortcut to find great deals.

- A great house flipping resource I just found.

- More ways to find great deals, less bad deals.

- Here's your house flipping checklist.

How about copy that uses **curiosity-inducing bullets** from Fred's PQR2s?

- Helps you find great deals fast.

- Makes it easy to find the deals others missed.

- Gives you the keys to make high profit off virtually all the deals you decide to do.

- Three steps to avoid chasing deals that won't work.

- The real secret for how to have fun doing deals.

- Discover how to find high profit deals in any market.

- Stop worrying about buying a poison house that will destroy your business.

These are curiosity-inducing bullets that pull Fred in because it's using his exact language and targeting his interests and fear. Quite frankly, when you read those, there's not a single thing about what's in the product. That's okay, because that's how you use curiosity-inducing bullets. You will find out more in Secret #9: The Ultimate Bullet Formula.

By the way, when I finally understood Fred, that's when we created Funnel Scripts. When you know Fred and have Funnel Scripts, you can create any piece of sales copy you need. Funnel Scripts takes your Fred parts and helps you assemble them into fantastic copy with the click of your mouse.

Knowing Fred gives you all the building blocks you need to create amazing sales copy without spending years trying to master it. That's why you need to identify Fred. Figure out Fred's PQR2, and you have the keys to the kingdom when it comes to creating copy. Understanding Fred is the key to your success.

Summary:

- Know your audience better than they know themselves.

- Pay as much or more attention to psychographics as you do demographics.

- Know Fred's PQR2.

- If you want a shortcut (or hack) use FunnelScripts. com to help automatically put all of this research and knowledge about Fred into your sales copy faster than any other method.

Secret #9

The Ultimate Bullet Formula

"Copy is not written. If anyone tells you 'you write copy', sneer at them. Copy is not written. Copy is assembled. You do not write copy, you assemble it. You are working with a series of building blocks, you are putting the building blocks together, and then you are putting them in certain structures, you are building a little city of desire for your person to come and live in."
Eugene Schwartz

S ales copy bullets are the workhorse of any copy. They are called bullets from the term "bullet point" which is a dotted list on the page or screen, typically 3-12 at a time. You see them on everything from Amazon listings to long-form sales letters to email teasers to brochures. You use bullets to arouse curiosity and give people reasons to take whatever action you want. That action could be anything from ordering or signing up or calling on the phone. Bullets:

- Build curiosity so you can create pressure inside people to get them to buy faster.

- Grab people's attention so you can address their specific wants (and needs) to make more sales.

- Convey important information quickly so you can get your message across fast to maximize every advertising dollar you spend.

The interesting thing is that when most people create bullets, they only include features. For example, if it's a drill, they'll say, "Hey, it's 18-volts, and it'll take up to an inch bit." Like that means something to somebody! Features are what we would put under "technical specifications."

The problem is people don't buy because of features. Features are how they compare things. **People buy the benefits**. What are they going to get as a result of that feature? You've got to understand the difference between features and benefits.

A feature is what something *is*.

A benefit is what something *does for* you.

We'll take the drill example. It's 18-volts, which is the feature. But what that feature *does* is enable you to drill through hardwood like butter so you can drill a bunch of holes without recharging the battery every five minutes.

The fact that it will take up to a one-inch bit (the feature) means you can do all types of projects, especially around your home, without having to switch tools (the benefit).

Again, understand the difference between features and benefits. Features don't make somebody buy something. The benefit of those features gets them to buy from you.

You don't need a thousand bullets in your copy. Depending on the copy job, I would take four, five, six, a dozen excellent bullets over a fifty crappy bullets.

Bullets have different functions in sales copy. You can put two or three at the top of a sales letter right under the headline to suck people in. You can use bullets in the description of a product, whether you're selling it on Amazon or your website or in an email. Bullets are what carry most of the weight of your copy. Once your headline pulls them in, you can use bullets to:

- Summarize what people will see in a video.

- Give people a preview of your blog post.

- List the benefits.

- Give people reasons to keep reading and to make a decision.

- Summarize what they are buying.

- And much, MUCH more!

If you don't learn how to use bullets, then you will have a problem creating the curiosity you need to drive people forward in the sales process. You won't build the pressure that gets people to buy.

Here's a quick story about using bullets to sell something.

That sales letter I mentioned in the Introduction to this book that has done over a million and a half dollars in $29 sales is for an e-book. To help boost sales through that letter, I used a list of bullets that corresponded to specific page numbers in the book. So for someone reading the bullets about "What's in the book?" it feels tangible because I'm telling them things like:

- How to get up, running, and selling on Amazon Kindle–FAST! (The Web's #1 e-book retailer WANTS to sell your e-book for you–here's how!) (Page 14)

- The *sure-fire* secret to creating an e-book that sells like crazy while having more fun than you ever thought possible! (Page 23)

- How to quickly avoid the #1 Mistake authors make that causes them to take months or years to write a book . . . so you can finish in just a few days. (Page 7)

- A step-by-step explanation of how to actually get a complete REAL e-book DONE in less than 72 hours! (Page 103)

- The absolute "bullet-proof" best e-book to write and sell online–FAST. (Page 2)

I've done this with video products, too. You can write bullets that provide the time stamp on specific videos to get the promise.
So bullets

- Give people a reason to act.

- Build curiosity.

- Carry the load of explaining what your product is and what it will do for them.

I think the all-time truism about features and benefits is only partially correct. You've probably heard the old saying, "people don't buy the drill; they buy the hole." Well, I think you need to drill down deeper than that! What they want is not the hole in the wall; they want their wife to stop bitching at them because they haven't hung that picture yet. They want their kid to be happy because they were able to put the nice neat hole in the front of the birdhouse or make the holes to bolt the jungle gym together.

What we need to drill down to is the *meaning* of each benefit.

So, here's my go-to formula for creating bullets. You've seen it already in this secret and probably didn't realize it.

Basic Bullet Formula

Formula: It _____ so you can _____

Remember, Feature = what it is and Benefit = what it does.

Now, I'm sick of drills, so let's switch to something sexy. Let's talk about wrenches! Here are some bullets I wrote for a set of Dewalt wrenches I've been eying on Amazon for $29 but can't seem to pull the trigger to purchase. I guess I'm just not emotionally attached to them yet!

Here's the original bullet list from Amazon:

- **One-piece set**
- **SAE sizes**
- **Chrome vanadium steel construction**
- **Stamped markings for easy wrench size identification**

Yawn. Not very compelling. But I want to want these wrenches, so let's give them some help, shall we?

- One-piece set *so you can* keep all your wrenches together in one place

- SAE sizes *so you have* the exact size you need when you need it

- Chrome vanadium steel construction for strength and durability *so you can* work them hard

- Stamped markings for easy wrench size identification *so you can* quickly find the right size

Already we've made a difference. That's better than 80% of people do with their bullets just by adding the benefit. But we want to do better than 99% of people out there, and that's where my Ultimate Bullet Formula comes in. Are you ready?

Feature + Benefit + Meaning

Feature = what it is

Benefit = what it does

Meaning = what it *means* to the buyer / reader / prospect

Formula: It _____ so you can _____ which means _____.

FEATURE
+
BENEFIT
+
MEANING

So let's light those wrench bullets on *fire* and make even the most inept dad with six thumbs on one hand believe he can finally be the mechanic he always dreamed. A real "honey-do-list" house pro! Are you ready?

- **One-piece set so you can keep all your wrenches together in one place *which means* you'll never be left high and dry with the wrong wrench**

- **SAE sizes so you have the exact size you need when you need it *which means* you can get projects done faster and move on with your life**

- **Chrome vanadium steel construction for strength and durability so you can work them hard *which means* you'll spend a LOT less money on tools over time**

- **Stamped markings for easy wrench size identification so you can quickly find the right size**

which means no more pulling your hair out over stripped nuts

When you start talking about benefits and meaning, your sales copy bullets (and your sales copy in general) will take a quantum leap in effectiveness. And when you start *thinking* in terms of benefits and meaning, the sky is the limit as far as your selling power is concerned.

So, as we wrap up this secret, when writing bullets, get the momentum going. It's kind of like headline brainstorming. As you make bullets, you'll have ideas pop into your head for other bullets. As you focus on the different features, benefits, and meanings of whatever it is you're selling, your bullets will get better and better. It's kind of like warming up from a run or exercising where the third or fourth or fifth set is when you get into a groove. Your first bullet isn't nearly as good as your fifth, sixth, or tenth!

Also, if you need five or six bullets, write ten or twelve and choose the best five or six. Again, it's just a game of momentum. And one last thing. You can build up a very effective swipe file for bullets. I would highly recommend you start creating a clip file of bullets you see that catch your attention. Just like having a swipe file of headlines, having a swipe file of bullets can come in handy when you need to brainstorm a bunch of them quickly.

Summary:

- Bullets are the workhorse you use to create curiosity in your copy.

- Five amazing bullets will outperform 30 good bullets.

- Always include meaning in your bullets because that's the secret sauce that makes them better than everyone else's bullets!

Secret #10

What REALLY Sells People (It's NOT What You Think)

"There are two motives to action:
self-interest and fear."
Napoleon Bonaparte

"When dealing with people, remember you are
not dealing with creatures of logic,
but creatures of emotion."
Dale Carnegie

This secret is about the why and how to get people to react with emotion, because emotion is what drives sales. It takes the previous secret about bullets to the next level. How? Well, we talked about features and benefits. Features are what something *is* (it's got an 18-volt drive motor; half-inch drill bit capacity; it's a 30-minute real-time exercise DVD, etc.). The benefit is what that feature *does for* somebody. Meaning is what those features and benefits combined *mean* to someone.

They know the benefit of the 18-volt drive motor is that it gives you more power and you never run out. You're never at a loss to do your projects. But that last step is the most critical. You need to tell people about the outcome.

Meaning creates emotion.

The 18-volt drive motor has all the power to handle any project.

What does that mean to my ideal prospect?

In fact, you need to ask that question about *any* claim or feature or benefit you present to people in your sales copy.

It could mean your wife is happy you'll get the honey-do list done quickly. It means you'll burn through every job with enough time left to sit down on the couch and watch the football game. It means you'll see the smile on your kid's face when you finish up that project you're doing together. It means you'll have some more free time this weekend instead of waiting for the battery to recharge.

Meaning is the next level of connecting with people on a gut level about what your product, service, software, etc. will do for them, which is where people buy. Because you may have heard "people buy on emotion and they justify on intellect"—and that is *true*!

How do you find the meaning? Easy! Every time you see a claim, feature, or benefit, ask yourself some questions: "*Why* is that important?" "Why does that matter?" "Why is that a big deal?"

Now you might ask, "Why would I want to make a drill emotional?" And my response is if you sell drills and want to sell a lot of them, get people emotional about the drills. Make them feel cool by owning that drill. Make them feel smart by having that drill. Make them feel like they're a member of the tough-guy-club or popular by owning that drill. Make them feel like they love their kid by having that drill.

Do that, and you'll sell more drills!

By the way, this idea of injecting emotion through meaning applies to anything you sell, which is why it's important. Emotion is what sells. You have to drill down (pun intended) to that emotion, find it and expand it.

Now you might be saying, "Man, that's stretching it."

Is it? When I say, "The drill has a magnetic plate on the front so you can keep screws secure while doing your job. That means there's no chance of those sharp screws dropping and hitting somebody on the head while you're ten-feet up on a ladder. That one feature could keep someone from getting a screw embedded in their head . . . maybe even your kid."

Again, you might think that's a little bit of a stretch, but it's not! You've got to drill down to that emotion tied to each one of those features. The cool thing, it's just like taking those bullets or any other claim and doing that first part of the formula "It _____ so you can _____." Now you're dimensionalizing the product. Now, you're getting to the part that's going to get people to say, "Yeah, that's what I want to *feel*. That's what I care about. I don't care that it's blue, or it's got this logo on it, but I want my kids to be safe. I want my wife to be happy. I want to be able to relax. I want to get this damn honey-do list done so I can sit down and watch the game and fall asleep and spill nachos all over the front of my shirt."

That's what this drill means. As soon as you can make that connection, your sales will get pumped up! The consequences of not doing this are severe. If you can't connect on an emotional level, then you're the same as everybody else. Then people evaluate your product, coaching, software, or whatever you sell based on price alone because that's all they have to go on. You haven't made them feel anything! But as soon as you make them feel something, that's when you have them. They need a powerful WHY if you want them to buy because **WHY creates emotion.**

Now, I'll tell you a quick story.

Here's the reason I signed up to do physical coaching with a guy named Stew Smith. He sends me workouts through email, even though I've been working out already and own plenty of books with exercises. Stew lets me call him on the phone and ask him questions about workouts, but I had other people I could call for free. The reason I initially signed up with him was the emotional motivation of, "Hey, my trainer is a Navy SEAL. That's pretty badass!"

Initially, I enjoyed the emotional ego hit of telling people, "Hey, my personal trainer is a Navy SEAL." And I let that slip every once in a while, maybe more than I should because it is pretty cool. But here's the interesting thing.

That emotionally charged reason for signing up with Stew got me motivated enough that, now in my 50s, I'm in better shape than most 25-year-olds. (I can do 33 pull-ups, 100 push-ups, and 100 sit-ups in a row without stopping.)

All because of that emotional connection to my trainer being a Navy SEAL, I'm

A) Not going to let him down by slacking on workouts.

B) Not going look like Mister Potato Head ever again, especially if I want to tell people my trainer is a Navy SEAL.

That emotional reason for signing up/buying/clicking has all types of consequences for your sales funnel as far as your prospect is concerned. You've got to find that emotional connection and amplify it. The more emotions you can tie your product or service to like love, fear of _____, hate, and hope, the better off you are.

Putting this into action is super easy. Here's the trick.

As soon as you make a statement about what something *is* or what it *does*, you use those two magic words "which means _____."

". . . which means you will _____."

". . . which means you will be able to go sit down and relax."

". . . which means you can _____."

". . . which means you can enjoy spending more time with your family."

". . . which means you don't have to _____."

". . . which means you don't have to waste an entire Saturday doing chores."

That's how you do it. That's how you find the meaning. And the more emotionally charged you can make that meaning, the more sales you'll make! Tie your product to:

- Love for _____ (family, self, country, community, etc.)
- Hate
- Fear of _____ (failure, making mistakes, death, loss, etc.)
- Vanity
- Pride
- Longing for _____ (fulfillment, peace, completion, etc.)
- Greed
- Freedom

Tie your product or service to the things people want at their core, and you'll be able to connect emotionally much more quickly.

Now that you're conscious of this, you need to use this knowledge to your advantage. You need to include this emotional component in the mix. As soon as a feature comes out of your mouth, imagine a customer asking you "Why?"

"Why is that important?" "Why should I care?" "Why does that matter to me?" "What does that mean to me?" Almost like an annoying child who just snorted a Pixie Stick at midnight on Halloween who now has a case of "why-a-rhea!" Imagine that incessant, why, why, why, why, why, and it'll force you to come up with the answers.

Again, it's one of those things where you build momentum. Write out ten, twenty, or thirty reasons why a feature or benefit matters to them. It is that important to your business and your ability to create awesome copy. Find that emotional connection.

Now the truth is, when you do this exercise, you don't find the emotional connection with the first thing you write down. It happens after you work your way through the easy ones and force yourself to keep going. When you get past the superficial level and start drilling down below the surface, then you will tap into the true emotions.

Emotional connection is how you turn lookers into buyers. It is how you turn buyers into raving fans. And, it is how you turn raving fans into customers for life!

So that's the secret to what really sells people. It's not what *you* think . . . it's what *they* feel.

Summary:

- People buy on emotion and then justify with logic.

- The primary emotional motivations to buy are fear and desire.

- You should strive to make an emotional connection with your prospects and buyers by tying your product or service to as many different reasons why as you can.

Secret #11

Why Good Enough Makes You (and keeps you) Poor!

"The Enemy Of Great Is Good!"
Unknown

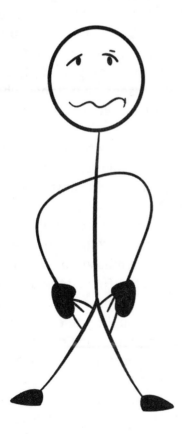

One of my early mentors was a successful real estate agent. Some people thought he was pompous. Part of the reason was that he would not accept anything other than total excellence. He had a sign on his door that said, "The Enemy Of Great Is Good!"

That always stuck with me. When something is good enough, it will never be great. How does this apply to sales copywriting? When a piece of sales copy works, we tend not to want to touch it because we get superstitious or scared. We know it took effort and work to get it to this point where it's making us money. The fear is that if we change the copy it will "break" and stop working (and maybe not start working again when we change it back)!

Let's say, for example, that for every dollar you spend you bring in $1.10 or $1.20 or $1.52. So it's good enough, and you don't want to mess with it. (Hey, you're making 50% profit!) But that mindset keeps you poor. Only once in 25 years of writing copy have I seen an instance where the original headline and the original copy could never be beaten.

Usually, you find a way to make it better using a simple process called A-B split testing. A-B split testing means you take something that's working and test it against something else you hope will give you a better result.

Here's how this works. You have two versions of your copy: the A version and the B version. You run the test for a while (preferably a test tied to a measurable result like total sales, clicks, subscriptions, etc.) Then, if the B version beats the A version, the B version becomes the new A version. Now you have a champion you'll try to outdo with a new version. They call this champion "The Control."

So A/B split testing tries to constantly improve your best copy and make it convert better.

Refer back to the example in Secret #6 where I changed a headline, and my sales increased from zero sales to ffive sales in two minutes (a 500% increase). Another example in the Introduction talked about changing a website from 20 pages to one page and sales increased by 250%.

What if I hadn't made those changes? Would you be reading this right now? Hell no! I'd still be living in the trailer park delivering newspapers. If I had not made those changes, we never would have made the money that we made. My life would have been completely different.

So it's critical that once you've got something working, you *must* test to make that copy better. Little incremental improvements can produce massive profitability.

$100 Product Example

For example, you have a $100 product for sale with a 1% conversion rate on your sales letter.

That means you make $100 for every 100 visitors who come to your website. (100 visitors x 1% conversion = 1 sale at $100).

Let's say it costs you $90 to get 100 visitors to your website resulting in one sale. (I'll assume you're selling an e-book or something with no physical delivery costs.)

That means you spent $90 on traffic. You made $100 in sales. Your gross profit is $10.

Now, let's start testing.

You test your headline and increase your conversion from 1% to 1.2%. That measly little .2% increase in conversion can't mean much, can it? On the contrary, for every 100 visitors that come to your website, you're now making $120, but you're still just spending the same $90 (your cost didn't go up).

You just tripled your profitability! How? Instead of making $10 profit, you're now making $30 profit. Same traffic. Same advertising expense. With this simple headline test, you tripled your profitability.

What if you tested a few of the bullets and raised conversion by just 0.1%?

What if you tested the offer itself and raised conversion by 0.15%?

What if you tested a simple picture at the top of the page and raised conversion by 0.25%?

Now you're converting at a rate of 1.7%. Nothing else has changed in your costs, but you've increased profits by 700% ($70 profit vs. $10 profit)! Hey, you're making $170 for every hundred visitors instead of that stinky $100 you were so happy with before you started testing.

This process can be repeated multiple times once you understand it needs to be done and have the courage to do it. The funny thing is, it doesn't take courage to do it! Why? Because if you try a new headline and it doesn't do as well, you turn it off. It's not like you're a loser if it doesn't work as well as the first version. Go back to your original champion and start looking for a new challenger!

My friend Russell Brunson's book *108 Split Test Winners* details over 100 tests his company did to explode profits, skyrocket sales, and create an avalanche of subscribers. You can get the book for FREE (you only pay shipping and handling) here https://CopywritingSecrets.com/freesplittestingbook

By the way, all this testing used to be super complicated and technical to do which is why few people did it. But now, with incredible tools like *ClickFunnels*, it is easy to implement A-B split testing. There are plugins, software, and services out there that make it inexpensive to test. It's easy to set up, and you *must* do A-B split testing with everything, including:

- Headlines

- Offers

- Prices

- Bonuses

- Email subject lines

- Calls to action

- Order button text

- Colors

You can test all of these and more. However, here's the number one thing you need to understand:

You never test more than one variable at a time.

If you're going to test a headline, test one against another, but everything else on the page stays the same. If you're going to test the text on your order button, that's all you're testing and everything else on the page stays the same.

As soon as you start changing more than one variable at a time your test results become invalid.

Use a tool to automate the testing process. Whatever you're using for your website, see if there is a built-in A-B split test feature. If not, then go out and *find* a tool. Do a Google search for "A-B split testing tools" and find tons of options.

Your takeaway on this secret is this: Start testing.

Start! Test one thing at a time. Don't accept the results you're getting now are as good as it's going to get. Think about it. Most retail businesses are operating at a 10% profit margin. Imagine! By doing a simple test on your website, your flyers, and your ads, you increase conversions by a tiny % and explode your profits. What would that mean to your business and your family? For many thin-margin companies, it's totally life-changing!

So much hidden profit is right there waiting for you, just by testing a few simple things. You can't afford *not* to do this!

Summary:

- If you're not testing, start testing immediately.

- Never test more than one variable at a time.

- Test for actions like purchases, clicks, or subscriptions.

- Automate your testing. Don't do it by hand if at all possible.

Secret #12

Don't Reinvent The Wheel— Great Copy Leaves Clues

"Your job is not to write copy. Your job is to know your visitors, customers and prospects so well, you understand the situation they're in right now, where they'd like to be, and exactly how your solution can and will get them to their ideal self."
Joanna Wiebe

You need to do the right research before you start creating your sales copy. Why? So you're immersed in the mindset of the people you're targeting with your sales message. Now, what type of research would you need to do? What do you need to know?

What do they want more than anything?

What are their big desires? What are their fears? What scares them? What are their objections to buying stuff like what you're trying to sell?

You need to find out these things:

- What do they want?

- What are their fears?

- What are their objections to buying either what you sell or what anybody is selling out there?

If you do that, you have a massive advantage over the other people creating sales messages.

Look at the sales messages your customers see in the marketplace. Look at the number one bestselling books on Amazon that target your audience. Read the back cover copy. Look at the chapter titles. See the sales messages used to get these people to buy.

This process is called "funnel hacking." Look at what's already working with an offer, sales copy, and product, then apply that to what you're doing with your products and services. You don't steal what others are doing, but you do model how they're approaching and selling to the marketplace.

Where do you research?

Amazon is my number one source for research. Not only can I see what people are buying since Amazon has everything listed in categories of best sellers, but I can also look at the comments that people make and their feedback (or lack of feedback) on every product. I read the five-star reviews to see what gets people excited.

More importantly, I read the one-star reviews to see what has people pissed off and make sure I don't do that with my offers.

But the real gold when you're looking at reviews is in the two, three, and four-star reviews. Why? Because those are the people who liked some of it and didn't like other parts. Those are the most helpful people because, quite frankly, the five-star people are often fanboys and the one-star people are just bitter "know-it-alls" who hate life. The two, three, and four-star people explain, "Hey, it did this, which was good, but it didn't do this, which upset me."

Use their words to help write your sales copy.

Let's say you're selling a product about how to speak Spanish. You notice people complain that a popular product doesn't teach you conversational Spanish. Instead, it sounds like you're learning straight out of a classroom.

Here's how you can use that feedback.

1. Clue yourself in on what to include in your own product.

2. Emphasize how your product uses conversational Spanish.

3. Use that angle in your headline, "How To Learn Conversational Spanish In As Little As Two Weeks!"

Those are the things you find out when you do the research. You have to immerse yourself in the sales messages potential customers are seeing and how they react to them.

Google is another great research resource. If I want to solve a problem, I'll search Google to see what comes up. Read the blog posts, look at the ads, look at the keywords people use and the related products. Look for the ideas people share in blog posts and articles. Look at the questions people ask. It might take a couple of hours or a couple of days to immerse yourself. It might take you a week, depending on your schedule and how well you know your audience. But it'll be the most valuable couple of hours, couple of days, or week that you ever spend. This research is how you see the words people use and connect with them in your sales copy.

The consequences of not doing this are severe. Quite frankly, if you don't use the words they use, if you don't resonate with them, they will not buy from you. Your sales messages will fall flat with your target audience. They won't pay attention to your headlines. If they do pay attention to your headline, then your copy won't work and your ads won't be any good.

Immersive research helps you pretend you are one of your prospects with the same problems and desires. See what's available out there. Look at the sales messages and the feedback, especially for products and services that are popular with your target audience.

Immersive research gives you a direct way to take advantage of where your competitors are succeeding *and* where they're failing. It automatically positions your offer as a unique and better solution just by understanding the market through research.

Feedback from one of my products brought this home to me in a big way. For almost two years I had the number one PowerPoint educational DVD on Amazon. We sold thousands of this thing. While looking at the feedback, I realized that some people felt like the entire DVD was a pitch for a piece of software called Snagit®. I thought, «What the hell are you talking about? I demo how to create a PowerPoint presentation with all these different slides, and I use Snagit as the example to build the presentation around. I don't care if you ever buy Snagit. I don't even tell you where to get it!"

But it shows that people don't pay attention! (Big surprise there.) They'd buy the DVD and watch it, but they didn't pay attention to the slides I made using Snagit as the example. They skipped ahead and watched the part of the training where I showed the final presentation which happened to be an excellent presentation for Snagit! But if they had watched the whole instructional video, they would have seen that I built the presentation in front of them.

This confusion never occurred to me, but I changed some verbiage and part of the sales copy which cleared it up. It's a great example of why you want to look at the feedback from your competitors. However, you also look at your feedback to improve your own sales copy.

My competitor could have exploited this issue to their benefit by saying something like, "And unlike other training, we don't try to sell you anything extra. We include everything you need to make amazing PowerPoint presentations and don't pitch any extra software." Even though it was BS, and I wasn't pitching, a competitor could have smoked me if they'd been paying attention.

Another place to do research is your frequently asked questions that come in, or your email support tickets. Those are a goldmine. Nobody wants to read the negative feedback or objections, but if it makes you a whole lot wealthier, then that's enough motivation to do it.

When you sit down to write your copy, research needs to be part of your planning process. Say, "Hey, I've got to write a sales letter, a postcard, or an email. Let me designate a couple of hours to do some research. If I'm selling a book, let me research popular books. I've got to write a sales letter for my software, let me go research software." Make this part of the copywriting process. Instead of opening your word processor and staring at the blank blinking cursor, wondering what to write, do some research! Get your mindset in the right groove, and some amazing copy will result.

As I've said before, writing copy is a game of momentum. You need to get your copywriting engine warmed up before you write. Kickstart that process by reading other people's text and the feedback from customers on the related things they buy. This practice gets you into that copy mindset and makes it easier to start writing.

My best piece of advice about the research before writing sales copy is:

1. Just do it. Get the words, feelings, and ideas directly from sales copy that engages people.

2. Understand the reactions of people. Amazon and other sites that allow you to look at reviews are your goldmines.

Spending a few hours researching similar products helps you get into the flow of creating sales copy. The result is better sales copy, written *much* faster.

Summary:

- Never write sales copy without doing research.

- Research gives you the words and the intel you need to write better copy.

- Only a fool sits down at the keyboard and starts writing copy cold without warming up first.

Secret #13

It's All About Them—Never About You

"Simplicity is the ultimate sophistication."
Leonardo Da Vinci

*"Make it simple. Make it memorable. Make it inviting
to look at. Make it fun to read."*
Leo Burnett

Once you talk to your audience, you tend to want your audience to see how smart you are. You use industry jargon or big words. You want them to know you know what you're talking about. This tendency happens no matter what you're selling.

If you're selling a drill, you start talking about voltage and torque.

If you're selling a coaching program, you talk about your 25 years of experience and how you know these cool things.

If you're selling software, you talk about gigabytes and use hard-to-pronounce words.

However, you actually prove to people how smart you are by communicating with them in a way they can understand! When they can still track with you despite being harried, confused and only partly paying attention, that's when you prove how smart you are. You do that by making it all about them.

Making it all about them means you avoid being cute, using sarcasm, inside jokes, or using anything that could be misconstrued.

You avoid trying to prove how smart you are by using big words, industry jargon, or acronyms you don't explain. All that does is confuse people and turn them off.

One thing I've learned in sales is that a confused mind always answers "No!" Someone who's confused never agrees to buy. Maybe one in a thousand does, but you usually can't make money off of one in a thousand.

When you are making a sale that involves a lot of emotion with a person who is scared, feels self-conscious, believes they're going to get ripped off, or is afraid of making a mistake, it is critical that your communication is crystal clear. Be very conscious of what you say to people.

In the mortgage business, we learned to talk about complicated financial stuff in a way that made sense to people who didn't want to understand what we had to disclose. For example, one thing we had to reveal was the high probability that the servicer of their loan would transfer to another party, but the principal was still owed, and the interest would never change.

I took two pages of complicated disclosures and just explained, "The company you make your mortgage payment to will most likely change. The only effect that has on you is who you make the check out to each month and where you send it." It was so effective at cutting down people's anxiety that the VP of the mortgage company had me do a training for the other loan officers on how to do disclosures.

That's when I really learned to use words my target audience understood to help them make a good decision. The consequences of not doing this is making people feel stupid.

- If you make somebody feel stupid, they won't buy from you.

- If someone feels like you're making fun of them or talking down to them, they won't buy from you.

- If they feel like you're too smart for them to understand, they won't buy from you.

- If you talk in circles and they get confused, they won't buy from you.

So you need to use the words they use.

- You need to talk in simple terms they understand.

- You need to use short sentences.

- You need to keep your thoughts well-organized and sequential.

If you can do that, you'll serve them better and help them achieve the result you're trying to sell to them.
Don't use big words.
Whenever I write something that has the potential for confusion, my secret strategy is to give it to my street-smart

wife. She was a 911-dispatcher for seven years and then worked the front desk at the police department for five years. She's been there, done that, and seen it all as a great student of humanity. The good news is that she didn't graduate from college. All she knows to do when software doesn't work is to yell for me to come to her office and fix it.

These qualities make her the perfect person for me to give a piece of copy and ask, "Hey, would you read this and tell me where it's not clear? Where it doesn't make sense?" She's excellent at that. I've used my mother for that role as well.

Find somebody who doesn't know what you know and get them to read your sales copy and see if they understand it. If they can understand it, then you're on the right track. And no, they don't have to be a member of your target audience to be an effective sounding board for your sales copy. In fact, it often helps if they aren't.

I've also heard people say to give your sales copy out to a bunch of people, and if they come back to you and say, "Ah, it's pretty good," that means it's not good at all. Why do these experts say that? Because what they want is for everybody who reads it to say, "Wow, that sounds cool. Where can I get one?" If people come back and say, "Hey, it's pretty good," then you still have work to do on your copy.

Now, of course my wife's not going to buy anything I'm selling, so that's not a good litmus test, but you get the idea. Also, unless the people you hand the copy to are in your target audience, they aren't EVER going to say "Hey, where can I get one?" So that old saying only holds so much water in my book.

If I had to boil all this down to one big takeaway, it's this: Write or create your sales copy so it speaks directly to your ideal prospect.

Write to a single person; don't write to a group. Write to someone you know who represents the perfect person in your target audience (remember Fred from Secret #8). This trick works exceptionally well when you are stuck.

True story: My buddy George, represents my audience. If I'm stuck writing a sales letter, video sales letter, or any piece of copy, then I say, "Hey George, I've got something you need to hear about."

Writing to George works well for e-mail teasers because I have a tendency to get detailed in my emails and make them fifty pages long when they only need to be five lines. When I find myself doing that, I'll throw it all away and just start typing an email to my buddy, George.

> Subject: Cool software I just found
>
> Hey George,
>
> I just found this cool piece of software.
>
> I know you're really interested in _____ and this is really neat.
>
> You want to check it out because it does this, this, this, and this.
>
> Here's the link. LINK
>
> I'll talk to you soon.
>
> Bye.
>
> Jim

Emails you compose as if to a specific person will out-perform everything else 99% of the time.

Always remember that millions might read your sales message, but you're selling to one person at a time.

Talk like them.
Use words they understand.
Never make them feel stupid!

Summary:

- A confused mind always answers "No" in a sales situation.

- Keep your messages simple and direct.

- Don't use big words and don't make people feel stupid.

- It's not about how smart you are; it's about how much you can help them.

Secret #14

What To Do If You Don't Have Any Testimonials Yet

"We have become so accustomed to hearing everyone claim that his product is the best in the world, or the cheapest, that we take all such statements with a grain of salt."
Robert Collier

"Do what you can, with what you have, where you are."
Theodore Roosevelt

So here you are. You've busted your butt and written your book, created your software, designed your service, or hung the sign on the door of your coaching business. But you don't have any testimonials yet.

Some people see this as a handicap they'll never overcome. People get hung up on this stuff because they see people using testimonials, feedback, endorsements, and reviews in their sales copy, but they don't have any yet.

Yes, testimonials can help you build momentum and improve the effectiveness of your sales messages. But when you're talking about sales copy and the sales process, what you're actually worried about here is **proof**. When most people read your sales copy, at some point their brain says, "Okay, sounds good. But why should I believe you? Will this work for me? Has this worked for other people? Do I really need this?"

Lack of proof is the real reason why you think you need testimonials and freak out if you don't have any.

Testimonials usually come in sales copy after you have made your claims and your offer. So, you've pulled them in with the headline. You've aroused their curiosity with your fabulous bullets. You've given them the information, and now all of a sudden it's time to start thinking about making that purchase decision. That's when many people will say, "Well, yeah, that sounds good, but I've heard this stuff before. Why should I believe you?"

You need proof that what you're talking about is significant and will work for them. There are many different proof elements you can use besides a product-specific testimonial.

In an ideal world, you would have a results-oriented testimonial which is from someone who used your product, service, or software, etc. The person got great results and are willing to say, "I used it. I got this result, this result, and this result. It was awesome and changed my life and here's proof."

Results-oriented testimonials are the types you want. But you have to be careful, especially in the areas of health, finance, banking, investing, and things like that. There are specific requirements for testimonials like that. There are disclaimers and disclosures you need to provide (you can investigate those on your own). But the authorities are particularly concerned with any claims made about health or finances.

Bottom line: be careful and never manufacture a results-oriented testimonial.

The next type of testimonial is about you and your company. These are relatively easy to get. You just ask people you've done business with or people who know you to provide a testimonial about you or your company so you can have testimonials on your website. Simply ask them what they would say to a friend or colleague about you and if it would be okay to put that quote on your site. It's that simple.

The next testimonial is a celebrity endorsement. The celebrity can be a notable figure in your niche world.

For example, in 2001, when I published the e-book that launched me into the online business arena, I received an endorsement from a gentleman named Jay Conrad Levinson who wrote the Guerilla Marketing books. I sent him a copy of the book, asked him if he'd say a couple of words about it, and he endorsed it. That was huge! By the way, you've got nothing to lose by asking people you don't know if they'll review your product. Send it to some people recognized by your target audience and see if they'll endorse you. Most of them won't, but you only need one or two to say yes to change your life!

After celebrity endorsements, the next thing you can use is statistics that support what you're telling people. There are tons of studies and statistics out there on anything you can imagine. Go to Google and enter your topic plus the word "statistics" or "study."

Here's an example: We want to find some proof to support the sales message for my book *Selling Your Home Alone*. You would go to Google and search for "for sale by owner statistics." According to the National Association of Realtors, nine out of ten for-sale-by-owners will fail, give up, and list with a real estate agent within thirty days. So you can play that up in the proof section and say, "The truth is, according to statistics, nine out of every ten for-sale-by-owners will fail. Don't let that be you. That's why you need this book!"

Leverage those statistics to give you the proof you need for the claims you're making.

You can also leverage quotes to help build your proof. Find some quotes that apply to what you're trying to get people to do or buy. Use those quotes in the appropriate places to instill trust and to reinforce the idea that to buy what you're selling is a good decision.

So if you don't have any testimonials yet, you now have a bunch of different options for getting proof elements into your sales copy.

Let me tell you a quick story.

One of the things I did to get testimonials for my first book, *Selling Your Home Alone*, was to give away copies of my book to people who were trying to sell their houses themselves. I handed it to them and said, "Here's my book. I think it will help you. If it does, would you mind giving me a testimonial? And please, let me know if you have any questions I can help you with."

That's all I said to them. Results? I received many testimonial letters for my book because I just gave it away and asked people to provide me with a testimonial.

How do you put this secret in action? Don't let the lack of testimonials hold you up. If you don't have results-oriented testimonials, then work your way down the different options I've given you. Find one or more to help you do what you need to do with proof.

The fastest way to get testimonials is to hand out something to different people and ask for a testimonial or an endorsement either for the product, for you, or for the topic in general.

Don't let the lack of testimonials stop you. People get all worked up and say stupid stuff like, "Oh, I don't have any of these things, so I won't be able to sell." That's not true. Will results testimonials help you sell more? More than likely, yes! But you can't sell more until you've sold some. And you can't sell some until you get the damn thing up there and offer it for sale in the first place!

Summary:

- Don't let lack of testimonials stop you.

- You need proof to help them feel comfortable making the decision to buy from you.

- Proof comes in many forms, including celebrity endorsements, statistics, and quotes that support your sales message.

- Give your product away to people in exchange for an honest testimonial.

Secret #15

3 Sales Formulas That Never Fail

*"If you don't sell, it's not the product
that's wrong, it's you."*
Estee Lauder

t is critical you understand Secret #8, your *Fred*, your avatar.

- What are his problems?

- What are his questions?

- What are his roadblocks?

- What are the results he wants?

Because if you don't understand Fred, you won't be able to use these formulas. So you've got to put in the research. An hour or two of proper research, understanding your *Fred*, and then following these three formulas is going to pay off not once, not twice, but for the rest of your life.

These formulas work for a 20-page sales letter, a one-minute video sales letter commercial, and a 10-minute sales talk. They work anywhere and everywhere for crafting sales messages.

Understanding how to structure a sales message.

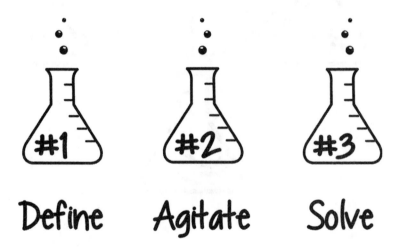

Define   Agitate   Solve

1. **Formula #1: Problem/Agitate/Solve.** This formula is my favorite because you can use it for anything. You construct your sales message in three parts:

   a. You *define* the problem they face

   b. You *agitate* it, make it worse, make it hurt

   c. You *solve* it by presenting your product or service as the solution

   Now, the key is to make it worse. A LOT worse! *Agitate* is the magic in this formula, which works for a 20-page sales letter, a one-page letter you might even send through the mail, or for an email. It works anywhere. You meet them with the problem they face, but don't leave it alone.

   Let's use dog aggression as our example.

   State the problem: "Here's the problem. If your dog barks or acts like it's going bite other people, this is something you need to get under control quickly."
   Agitate it. "If you don't, you could be subject to a lawsuit. Your dog could mutilate a child. You could carry the guilt as well as the financial burden of a single, instantaneous dog attack for the rest of your life. So no matter how innocent, cuddly, and friendly your dog is, if you don't have them properly trained, it could cripple you financially for the rest of your life." Remember, agitating is the secret sauce in this formula.
   Introduce the solution. You can say, "Luckily for you, there's now a solution. *The Complete A-to-Z Puppy-Dog Training Guide* helps you not only with aggression, but also with potty training, learning tricks, and socializing your dog to be a happy, healthy member of the family."

Boom. Whether that was a video sales letter directing somebody to a website from an email, a social media post, or a Facebook Live event, it doesn't matter. That's the formula: Problem/Agitate/Solve.

Let's look at another example: real estate flippers.

State the problem. "You want to flip real estate, but so does everybody else."

Agitate it. "To make matters even worse, every time one of those flipping seminars comes through town, a thousand people are fighting to find the deals you're out there every day trying to get. Which means, not only is it harder for you to be able to find deals, but also the deals you *do* find are getting thinner because all these newbies are willing to pay more money for these flips. So all the profit is gone out of the deal before you can even make the deal."

Introduce the solution. "Well, luckily for you, there's now a solution. It's *The Hidden Flippers' Detective* which helps you find the deals before they ever come on the market. It shows you how to find deals, how to finance deals, how to get deals done before anyone even knows there was a deal to be had."

Third example: marriage counseling.

State the problem. "You and your spouse don't talk the way you used to, and it may just seem like things are a little weird right now."

Agitate it. "But here's the real problem you're facing. If you don't reconnect now, statistics say there's a high probability that you'll end up in a divorce. Even if you don't, you'll live unhappily day-to-day, not with a lover, not with your best friend, but with a roommate. The only reason you're staying together is for the kids or to pay the mortgage."

Introduce the solution. "Well, luckily for you, there's now a solution, *The Marriage Revitalization Guide.* It helps you reconnect, keep communication open, and learn to appreciate each other again. It helps you reignite the fire that got you together in the first place. You'll become a team that takes on the world together. Get back to how you felt about each other before you got married."

Bam! Problem/Agitate/Solve. You can use it for anything and it works especially well with cold traffic.

2. **Formula #2: If you want 3X benefit, then do this.** This is a positive message bent. Use this when you're focusing on the desire and not a problem per se. You talk about benefit, benefit, and benefit, then whatever action you want them to take.

Let's look at the dog training example.

Instead of aggression, you want to teach your dog some cool tricks. It would be fun to have a well-trained dog that can do cool tricks. "So if you want to **train your dog, teach him some great tricks**, or even just **have a lot more fun with your pet**, then you need to check out *The 10 Tricks You Can Teach Your Dog In A Weekend* course. Here's why . . ."

Real estate investing.

"If you want to **find great deals**, if you want to **find deals before anybody else**, and you want to **create a steady stream of new deals you don't have to chase**, then you need to check out *Flippers' Paradise*. Here's why . . ."

Marriage counseling.

"If you want to **reignite the fire with your spouse**, if you want to **get back in touch with the feeling you had when you first got married**, or you simply want to **reconnect with your best friend in the world**, then check out *Marriage Revitalization Secrets*. Here's why . . ."

This second formula is that simple and usually works well with hot and warm traffic.

Before   After   Bridge

3. **Formula #3: The Before/After/Bridge**. This formula uses some NLP (Neuro Linguistic Programming—the study of how language gets people to take action).

a. **Start with the before.** Talk about the way things are now. Typically, there's a problem, a question, a roadblock, or something in the way that makes them unhappy.

b. **Introduce the after.** Tell them to imagine what their life will be like. In NLP, this is referred to as *Future Pacing.* "Imagine your life, circumstances, business, marriage, or whatever, once the negative is gone." Once you've painted that picture where they've solved the problem, answered the question, or removed the roadblock, they've gone from unhappy to happy. Now it's time to bridge your product to this happy feeling.

c. **Bridge**. "Here's the path to get there. Here's the product. Here's the service. Here's the method. Here's how you're going to bridge that gap of where you are now to where you want to be."

Let's look at our dog training example.

Start with before. "Your dog's not listening. You're worried that he'll get loose and run down the street, maybe even run into traffic and get hit. He might get in a fight with another dog. Or, he might bite a neighbor's child, which could lead to some serious legal problems."

Introduce the after. "Now, imagine what it would be like to have your dog listen to you. Not because he's scared of you but because he loves you. He walks with you down the street without a leash. Your dog does all kinds of fun tricks, and you enjoy your time together. You're not at all worried about your dog being aggressive or exhibiting any other negative behavior towards other people. And you're extremely happy together and have a great relationship."

Bridge. "Here's how you get to that point. It's called *Dog Training Secrets* which helps you get (this benefit), (this benefit), and (this benefit). Here's how . . ."

Real estate investing.

Start with before. Let's say your avatar has a question about finding deals. "Here's where you are right now. You can't find deals before everybody else does. You're hitting the classified ads every day. You're looking at Craigslist every day. You're pounding the pavement and looking at for-sale-by-owner signs every day. But the problem is everybody else is doing the same thing."

Introduce the after. "Imagine what your real estate investing life would be like if your phone was ringing off the hook with qualified people asking you to do business with them. You have unlimited sources of funding so you can do all the deals you ever wanted. You can cherry-pick the best deals for yourself, refer the rest to other investors, and get a finder's fee from every single transaction."

Bridge. "Let me show you how to do that. With *Flippers' Paradise*, you will be able to do (this), (this), and (this). Here's what I mean . . ."

Marriage counseling.

Start with before. "Here's the way things probably are right now. They're not too good; they're not too bad. They just are. You and your spouse pass each other in the hallway, you talk, you hug, occasionally you make love. But overall, things aren't the way they used to be, and you're starting to wonder why you are even together."

Introduce the after. "Imagine what your life would be like if every time you saw your spouse, you felt the same feelings you felt when you first met? When you courted? When you dated? And when you were together, it was the most special time you ever felt. You couldn't wait to see your spouse every night when you came home from work. You couldn't wait to spend time with them on the weekend and do things together."

Bridge. "Well, that doesn't have to be a fantasy. It can be your reality. And here's how to get there." Then you tell them how to achieve their goal with your product, service, etc. as the bridge to get them there.

This formula can work with all traffic temperatures!

Those are the three formulas. Where can you use them? Anywhere and for any purpose where you want to start selling. Use them in tweets. Use them in blog posts. Use them in social media updates or email teasers. These formulas work wherever you want to start the sales process.

Summary:

- These three sales formulas just plain work!

- These formulas take people through a mental process that sets them up to buy.

- Test each formula to find the one that works best with your audience.

Secret #16

It's All Ice Cream, But What Flavor Should I Choose?

"You can have everything you want in life if you will help enough people get what they want."
Zig Ziglar

W hen it comes to sales letters, you might ask, "What should I use: a video sales letter, a long sales letter, or a short sales letter? Which do you think is best?" Some people think that length matters.

To answer this question, I'll give you the personal answer followed by my professional answer.

Personal Answer

Start with a video sales letter. Why? For me, it's the fastest way to get an offer up when I want to test an idea, to sell something, to make an offer, or to launch a new funnel. Any time I go into the marketplace, a video sales letter is the fastest way for me to do this.

Here's how I structure the page.

- Start with the headline. Seems obvious, doesn't? But as we discussed in Secret #6, the headline is your most important piece of sales copy.

- Insert your video.

- Add a Buy button, placed right under the video.

In some cases, I will stop right here. In others, I'll add the following:

- Add 4-6 awesome, curiosity-inducing bullets under the buy button.

- Give the guarantee.

- Summarize what they'll get.

- Insert another Buy button.

- Closing copy.

- The Postscript (P.S.). Restate the main benefits stated in the video sales letter.

Now, it causes some people heartburn to have the video play automatically. In fact, there are an ever-increasing number of people online who rebel against videos playing automatically, and Google's Chrome browser has basically put the kibosh on auto-playing videos with the sound turned on.

Then, typically, we have a Buy button right under the video, followed by three to six bullets about the product, the software, the service underneath that. We sometimes flip those two, where we may have the video and then the bullets and then the Buy button, but typically my Buy button is going right underneath the video.

We have the guarantee and we have the summary of what they're going to get. So literally, in the summary we list off that they're going to get this, this, this, this, this, this, this, this and this (in a bulleted list). Then we have another Buy button. Finally, we have the close, and then probably a P.S. The P.S. basically just restates the main benefits expressed in the video sales letter itself.

That's the pattern I use for anything under a couple of hundred bucks.

Why this pattern?

1. It's quick. A video sales letter is a one-day project if you have the right tools and knowledge.

2. It's easy for people to digest. You run traffic to it, see how people react to it, and watch the results in sales, opt-ins, clicks, or whatever the objective is for your sales copy.

Does that mean long-form sales letters are dead? Absolutely not. Do not believe anybody who heralds the end of long-form sales letters. I still use them because they are effective.

Then why use the long copy if you start with video sales letters? You use the long copy to sell a higher priced item and if people need more information to make a purchase decision.

In my experience, nobody wants to watch an hour-long video sales letter. They'll attend an hour-long webinar, but they won't view a lengthy video sales letter. So, in some cases, you have to give people more information using long copy.

In a case involving higher priced stuff, they typically need more information, especially if it's a more technical sale. You have to give them more data so they can make a decision. This preference isn't a hard-and-fast rule. I know somebody who sells a $5,000 coaching program using an eight-minute video and no application process. You pay or don't pay at the end of the video.

Typically, the two reasons you use long copy are when what you're selling costs more, or people need more information to make a decision.

So in this case, typically what we'll do is start with a headline. We'll still do a sales video. Then we have the Buy button and then we have the long-form sales letter underneath all of that. So just because you're using the long-form sales letter doesn't mean that you don't use the video too.

By the way, it's okay if the long-form sales letter duplicates what you share in the video sales letter. In fact, I've actually seen where the video sales letter and the long-form sales letter were the exact same thing. The long-form sales letter was basically just a transcript of the video sales letter. Or, in other cases, the long-form sales letter was basically the script used to create the video sales letter.

Why would you want to have both the video and the long-form sales letter on the same page? Because people either watch the video, or they read the long-form copy. Also, let's say somebody's at work or in a situation where they can't or don't want to listen. They will read the copy. Some will even print it to read it offline. Some people want to read; some people want to watch. Some people will do both. In fact, some people will watch the video and then read the sales letter before they decide to buy or not.

When would you use a short-form sales letter? Typically, you would use it to sell something relatively inexpensive. You don't need a 30-minute video sales letter or a 30-page sales letter to sell something for 15 or 20 bucks. Typically, you're overselling if you use a longer sales message in those cases, and people can get suspicious.

You can also use a shorter sales letter or sales video with something that doesn't require a lot of explanation, such as a physical product. Simply hold it up in the sales video and say, "Hey, look. This is what I have. This is what it does. These are the benefits to you. Here's why you should buy this now."

Using a short sales letter makes sense when it's inexpensive and doesn't require a lot of explanation. If you did write longer copy, someone would say, "They're over-selling this product. Something is going on here."

Bottom line: My first option in 99.99% of the cases is a video sales letter.

Professional answer

Test which works better: a video sales letter, a long-form sales letter, or a short-form sales letter.

A word of caution: be careful of the *absolute experts*. These are people who tell you that something is only one way. Nobody knows for sure about anything until you test a video sales letter versus a long-form sales letter versus a short-form sales letter. Which type of sales copy to use is as much art as it is science for your specific audience.

The truth is, when people sell something, they find patterns that work for them and produce results. They assume the way they did it is always going to get results. Then they tell others this is the absolute only way to do it.

Let me give you an example. There was an internet guru who said red headlines don't work anymore. At the time, people believed your headline should be in red. But he told everybody, "Red headlines don't work anymore; your headline should be blue."

So everybody changed their headline colors to blue. And what happened? Many people's conversion rates went down. A few people tested red versus blue headlines (I was one of them) and found that red headlines out-performed the blue headlines on many of our sales messages.

Taken over thousands, tens of thousands, and hundreds of thousands of visits, the difference was remarkable. Those who didn't do any testing of this theory lost money because they took someone else's word for it that one way was better than another.

Learning patterns and formulas is good. But the only way to know what works is to test the different variants and see which one works best for your audience, traffic, and offer.

When you fall into a pattern because you did it before and got good results, be careful. That's when "good enough" kills your results. I have to be cautious of this all the time. When you keep doing it the same way and don't test, you end up potentially leaving a ton of money on the table.

One more example: Up-sells or one-time offers (offers made after the initial sale as part of a "sales funnel" to increase the overall profit per customer). I do these consistently now. Why? Because after ten years of selling the same product, I added a one-time offer to it, and immediately saw a 30% increase in profits. When that happened, I wanted to slam my head in a car door. Why? Because I saw the sales jump from the one-time-offer, mentally went backward ten years, and calculated all the money I had left on the table (to the tune of $980,000 over the years).

Bottom line: test to see if a video sales letter is going to work better than the alternatives. I recommend you start with a video sales letter using the above format. But you need to test what ultimately works best for you and your audience, so you know for sure what gets you the best results.

Summary:

- If in doubt, start with a video sales letter.

- In the end, you have to test long vs. short vs. video to find the best option.

- Beware of anyone who deals in absolutes when it comes to sales copy. The only way to know anything for sure is to test.

- Beware of falling into the trap of only doing things one way, especially if you've gotten "good" results from it in the past.

Secret #17

How To Write An Amazing Sales Letter—FAST

"The only purpose of advertising is to make sales.
It is profitable or unprofitable according
to its actual sales."
Claude Hopkins

Want to write an amazing sales letter fast? Then you need to learn the thirteen parts of a sales letter. I like to think of those thirteen parts as Legos, stacked one on top of another.

In this case, though, you go from the top down instead of from the bottom up when creating your letter. By focusing on the thirteen different parts, you don't feel the pressure to write an entire sales letter. All you do is create each of these parts in turn which makes it easier to complete.

Doing thirteen small steps is more attainable than doing one giant sales message project. You can spread these out as you have time, especially if you're a part-time entrepreneur.

Here's the key concept: The job of each part is to move people on to the next part of the sales letter.

Think of your sales letter as stepping stones across a stream. One stone leads to the next, to the next, and to the next. If you miss one, then someone's going to get wet and not make it to the other side where they will buy!

Another way to think about this is like an old fire bucket brigade. The fire truck pulls up with just a barrel of water. Then ten, fifteen, or twenty firemen pass the bucket filled with water one by one to the next person in line. If one of those firemen go down or gets out of line, the whole thing stops working and the building burns to the ground.

Bottom line: think about each of these parts in order, taking their turn passing the bucket.

Headline

The first thing is your headline package, which can consist of a pre-headline, headline, and sub-headline.
Example:

Attn: All Funnel Hackers

How To Get ALL Of Your Sales Letters, Scripts, And Webinar Slides Written (In Under 10 Minutes) WITHOUT Hiring An Expensive Copywriter!

(This Works Even If You HATE Writing And Never Want To Know ANYTHING About Copywriting!)

Just remember, the purpose of the headline is to attract attention from the right people.

Then, if you think about an actual letter, it's going to say something like "From the desk of," your name, and regarding the topic.

Example:

> *From the Desk of Jim Edwards*
>
> *Re: How to solve all your sales copy problems at the click of a button*

What have we done in that headline package? We've grabbed their attention, told them who the letter's from, and also told them what this letter is about in just a few words.

Now, in a video sales letter, what matters most are the first words that come out of your mouth.

Example:

> *Do you need to write an amazing sales letter? Hi, my name's Jim Edwards. In the next couple of minutes I'm going to show you how to write great sales copy fast.*

Your headline in a video sales letter or a spoken script are those first couple of sentences. So the first part grabbed their attention, then you identified yourself, and finally you let them know what to expect.

Shocking Statement

The second block is a shocking statement. Most people operate in a hypnotic state. They barely pay attention to what you're saying or what they're seeing or reading. Their mind is distracted by things like, "I should go check out Facebook;" "Hey, I wonder what's going on over on Twitter;" "Hey, I wonder what's for dinner tonight."

All these distractions assault their brains. Your job is to shock them, so they stop what they're doing and pay attention to you. You do this with a shocking statement or image. Now, it doesn't have to be something like, "Hey, let me flash you. Let me open up my trench coat," type thing. That would work for some sites! But in this case, a shocking statement might be something that goes against something they hold true or expose something they suspect is true.

Use a "Did you know?" statement.

For example:

> *Did you know most people who try to write a sales letter fail miserably? It's true. Some even go bankrupt and lose their houses!*

What?

Here's another:

> *Did you know the number one reason people get turned down for military service is not due to a criminal record but because they're considered too fat to train?*

And another:

> *Did you know that 99% of the people who start writing a book never finish, and they carry that regret like a 50-pound chain around their neck for the rest of their lives?*

Holy Crap. I better pay attention.

Now, here's a cool tip: Remember that research I showed you in Secret #14 to use if you don't have any testimonials? Well, often in that research, you'll find some cool information you can use for "*did you know*" statements.

Here are some examples for my for-sale-by-owner book. (I looked up "for sale by owner statistics" on Google just now.)

> *Did you know that nine out of every* ten for-sale-by-owners *are going to fail miserably and end up listing with a realtor within 30 days?*

> *Did you know the average for-sale-by-owner sells for over $59,000 **less** than homes sold by realtors?*

Oh, crap!

That's the reaction you want your reader or listener to have. You want them to STOP what they're doing and pay attention to every word you're sharing.

Define the Problem

Defining the problem uses a formula called *Problem, Agitate, Solve,* which we discussed in detail in Secret #15. Are there other formulas? Yes. Is this the easiest one to do? Absolutely. Is this the one that will most likely make you the most money quickly? You bet.

When you define the problem, you tell them in no uncertain terms the exact problem they face.

Here's the problem you face .

You can use that exact wording and fill in the blank. You state it in no uncertain terms.

Here's an example from the military fitness niche:

Here's the problem you face: as a society, we've become so sedentary that young people don't know how to get into shape and stay there.

Here's an example from the author niche:

Here's the problem you face: most people think that writing a book is so hard and takes so long they can't imagine becoming an author.

Agitate

You've told them the problem, but that's not good enough. You want to make it hurt because, the more it hurts, the more they need a solution and are willing to pony up with their time, money, and attention to solve it.

If you leave it at the problem stage, they'll say, "Well, I'm not *that* fat." Or, "I will finish my book when I get a chance." And then they lay their heads back down on the sofa, turn up *The Maury Show*, gorge on Cheesie Poofs, and never write their book.

"They don't buy if it don't hurt!" Jim Edwards

This step is where you pour on the *pain*. You make it worse by using a statement like, "which means you _____."

Notice this is the *same* statement used to elicit emotion in the Secret #9: The Ultimate Bullet Formula. However, instead of evoking a positive feeling, in this case, we use it to crush their soul!

Examples:

Which means you'll never get a chance to serve in the armed forces and serve your country.

Which means you'll struggle with being a fat couch potato for the rest of your life and never live up to your full potential.

Which means you'll never share your message with the world and when you die, your message dies with you.

You want them to say "Oh dang! That hurts. That stings. Okay, you got my attention. All right. I don't want to die like that. Save me now!"

This process does *not* have to take pages. It's a one-two punch in a bar fight they didn't know they were having! You smack somebody in the mouth hard enough, you've got their attention. You don't have to hit them again.

Present The Solution

Now you introduce them to your product or service that holds the solution they need to the problem you just made worse in the last step.

Once you've smacked them in the mouth and made it worse, say, "Luckily for you, there's now a solution. Let me introduce you to _____."

Examples:

Luckily for you, there's now a solution. Let me introduce you to the PT Test Survival Guide, *a brand new book to help everyone pass their next PT test.*

Luckily for you, there's now a solution. Let me introduce you to The Seven Day E-book, *the revolutionary course that helps anyone write and publish their own book or e-Book in less than a week, starting from scratch.*

That's all you have to do.

You introduce the solution with "Let me introduce you to _____."

Let me introduce you to my new coaching program.

Let me introduce you to an incredible piece of software that writes all your sales copy for you.

Let me introduce you to a quick-read book that will change your real estate investing life forever.

Whatever your thing is, this will work.

Use Bullets To Arouse Curiosity

This sixth block uses bullets to arouse curiosity. (See how everything you've been learning so far is coming together?) Once you've introduced the solution, take your features, benefits, and meanings and use them to build curiosity and desire for your solution.

How many bullets do you need? In my opinion, for most purposes, you need about six, eight, or ten rock-solid bullets. Nobody wants to read a hundred bullets. They need to see your six, eight, or ten best bullets. Am I saying you'll never use a massive list of bullets? No. But in the workaday world of sales copy, ten solid bullets pull the weight of fifty mediocre ones.

If you want to get good at bullets fast, review Secret #9: The Ultimate Bullet Formula.

Credibility Statement About You

Tell people about you and why you are qualified to bring them this solution. Again, depending on what piece of copy you're creating, this could be one sentence or a whole page listing your education, qualifications, and how you got to be where you are today. It depends on the length and purpose of your sales message.

If you need a long sales letter to sell a high-ticket item, where the sales copy carries the entire weight of the purchase decision, people will want to know the who, what, where, when, why and how of your qualifications to bring them this solution.

On the flip side, the guy who invented *The Perfect Push Up* and *The Perfect Pull Up* covered this credibility statement in a one-minute infomercial by saying, "invented by a Navy SEAL." Those five words were enough to establish all the credibility he needed to sell $100 million of fitness equipment.

Bottom line: answer the question, "Why you?"

Proof

Proof answers the question "Why should I believe you?" Use your testimonials and endorsements now. Use whatever you have at this point (statistics, quotes, government studies, etc.) to establish proof.

It's easy to introduce this by saying, *"But don't just take my word for it. Take a look at this."* That's always a great segue into this section.

One type of proof we haven't talked about is pictures or graphics. Images are one of the best forms of evidence, but they are also one of the most regulated. Why? Photos are compelling but are also easy to fake. Think about weight loss. The before and after picture is super powerful. Many of those pictures are fake. A dirty little secret is that the before (fat) picture is actually the *after* picture. In other words, people grab an old image of themselves when they were skinny, take a picture of themselves now as heavy, and then flip the pics. Nasty little trick! By the way, don't do this.

If you're making an income claim, you could show pictures of bank statements. People show pictures of checks all the time, especially in real estate investment sales copy. People will show pictures of people with whom they've done business.

My best advice: always tell the truth and back it up. If someone said, "Hey, you need to prove this is real in a court of law!" could you do it?

Sum Up The Offer And Give Price

In this section, tell them exactly what they're going to get, how they're going to get it, when they're going to get it, and how much it costs.

Coaching Example:

- This is a six-part coaching program that starts on this date

- It will be delivered weekly

- There will be time for Q&A

Drill Example:

- 18-Volt Drill

- Comes with bonus 20-piece drill and driver set

- Delivered via UPS and arrives in 3-4 days

Whatever it is, tell them exactly what they're going to get, when they're going to get it, how they're going to get it, and how much it costs.

Let's talk about pricing here. Some people who say you should do a dramatic price drop when you reveal the price.

In some cases, people are immune to that, especially if you are *not* selling in-person or on a webinar.

For instance, in a text ad or on a web page where you aren't present to close the deal, if you tell somebody, "Regularly, this is $399.00, but today you're going to get it for $2.50!" that's not going to work. Their BS detector goes off before they finish reading the sentence.

To see great examples of price drops for everyday product sales, look on Amazon. Virtually every single product they sell will have a regular price that's crossed out, and there's a reduced price. It's usually somewhere around a 10% to 30% discount. Also, look at the colors they use and how they cross out prices, etc.

You can say, "Regularly it is this price, but right now it's just this." You want people to feel like they're getting a great deal, and this is the place to do it.

Warning: Usually, those who live by the price die by the price. If the whole justification for buying what you sell is a low price, you'll rarely make money. Provide value pricing, but don't fall into *commodity* pricing where the price alone wins the battle. The cheapest guy in town rarely makes money (unless he's got one hell-of-a-back-end funnel)!

Bonuses And Pot Sweeteners

If you have bonuses, special savings, extra service included, or anything else to put them over the top, this is where you tell them about it.

In this section, you add more value to the offer. Maybe you throw in an extra something like a bonus report, an individual consultation with you, or anything that will make them feel like they are getting a fantastic deal on your offer. Be sure to build up the value of the bonuses and show why they are such a valuable addition to the offer.

Marlon Sanders, a man I deeply respect, told me something that caught my attention and has stayed with me for going on twenty years now. While standing in a hotel lobby in Boulder, Colorado in February 2001, he said, "Jim, the easiest thing in the world is to *sell dollars for dimes*." To increase the effectiveness of your offer, you pile on the bonuses until the total value of your offer is 10X the price you charge. That was cool advice.

Then Marlon said something that changed my life. To this day, I remember the Lipton tea bag tag hanging out of the side of his teacup as we stood there talking while all the attendee's at the event filed back into the meeting room. He and I were the only ones standing there when he dropped this knowledge bomb on me.

"Jim, if you really want to make your offer amazing, take your competitor's USP (unique selling proposition) and turn it into a free bonus with *your* offer."

In other words, whatever your competitors are offering that makes them unique, provide the same thing as a free bonus when people buy from you. That way, instead of comparing you to your competitors and trying to decide between the two offers, they buy from you because they see themselves getting everything they want without having to buy from anyone but you!

I could write an entire book on what that has meant to me over almost the last two decades, but I'll tell you what I immediately did with that new idea.

I was selling a mortgage education product that was doing okay. My main competitors at the time were mortgage software calculators. So I went and found a piece of mortgage calculator software I could buy the rights to and started including it as a *free* bonus with my offer. I told people they didn't have to buy a calculator from anyone else because I was giving one for free. My sales took off, and I never looked back.

CAUTION: Don't pile on a bunch of crap bonuses for the sake of piling on bonuses. Be strategic about it. Use those bonuses to create an offer that makes so much sense and feels so right people would be insane to say no.

Guarantee

The guarantee is where you take away the risk. Again, it could be a paragraph or a single sentence. You could simply say 30-Day No Questions Asked Guarantee. You might also do a guarantee where you restate every single one of the benefits you sold them on before.
Example:

> *Not only do we guarantee this unconditionally for 30 days, but if it doesn't show you exactly how to pass your next PT test, if it doesn't help you to get in shape in the next two weeks, if it doesn't give you a plan to get ready if you're not ready right now, we don't want your money. We'll give it all back. No questions asked. No hard feelings.*

Again, whichever way you do it, this is the time to take away all the risk.

Call Them To Action

You've told your buyer everything they need to know about the product. It's time to call them to action.
It could be a button that says, "Click here to buy now!" At this point, you can also give them another reason to buy right now. "When you order today, we'll give you another 10% off as part of a special marketing test."
If it's a big, long sales letter, you may recap all they'll get in a short bullet format.

- You're going to get the DVDs

- You're going to get the one-on-one coaching

- You're going to get instant access to the online training

- You're going to get the push-button software

- You're going to get the audiobook version

- You're going to get all my blueprints and templates

How you do this depends on what you're selling, what type and quantity of sales copy you're using, and where you are using it.

Postscript (P.S.)

The final part of your sales letter is the P.S. This is where you restate the benefits and tell them again to act now.

By the way, where did the P.S. come from?

Back when people wrote letters with quill pens or typed letters on typewriters, nobody wanted to rewrite or retype a whole letter if they forgot to include something important. That's where the postscript came from. It is the vital stuff you forgot to put in the letter, but you aren't going to retype the whole thing!

Here is where you restate the main benefits, the reason they should act now, and then you tell them to buy now! Example:

P.S. This gem will sell for $49. This introductory price of $29 is a "Buy it now before it's gone" offer, so act fast!

P.P.S. Let's be blunt: If you pass on this offer, in a week from today will you have an e-book written or not? Probably not!

*You'll still wish and want it, but you won't write it or make money from it. Face it. Most of what you need is instruction and encouragement. Get this book **now** and have your e-book as fast as one week from **today**! Wouldn't you like to be making money and bragging about your passive income within a week?*

Act now! Buy now! Your satisfaction is guaranteed. Click here!

This thirteen-step sales message formula will work for a ten-page sales letter or a one-page direct mail sales letter. Whether it's written on paper, displayed on the web, or delivered through video, these are the parts you must hit in the order given.

By following this thirteen-step process, you've addressed all their objections. You've solved all their issues by walking them through this psychological process of evaluating whether to buy or not. Each of these sections could be pages, paragraphs, sentences, or a few words. Remember to hit all the points, in order, if you want to make more sales.

Summary:

- The sales letter is like stepping stones across a pond—leave one out and you're going to stumble and get wet.

- This process works for a one-page letter, a video, or a twenty-page letter.

- Remember to stack up the value if you want people to buy from you.

Secret #18

How To Write Killer Email Teasers— FAST

"Good advertising is written from one person to another. When it is aimed at millions it rarely moves anyone."
Fairfax M. Cone

What is an email teaser?

An email teaser is an email that gets sent to either a single customer or a list of customers. You can send the teaser to your list, or you can entice an affiliate or friend to send it out to their customers and subscribers. **Ninety-nine times out of a hundred, the sole purpose of that email teaser is to get the reader to click a link in the email itself and go to a web page.**

The ability to write a great email teaser can make a huge difference in your business. The good news is, it's simpler than you might think. Once you understand the whole purpose of an e-mail teaser is to get somebody to click on a link in that email and go to a web page, your life gets a lot easier!

Most people make the mistake of selling the offer in the email teaser. Don't! Your sales letter or video sales letter will sell them.

The email teaser has one purpose: to get them to click to the website so they can:

- Read your sales message
- Watch your sales video
- Absorb your content
- Read your blog posts
- Watch your content video (which in turn refers them to your sales website)

The only purpose of an email teaser is to get a click and to prepare the viewer for what they will see once they click. Once you understand that, it's real simple.

There are only a few parts to a great email.

The first part is the subject line. The subject line serves the same purpose for an email as the headline serves on your sales message. Bottom line: If the subject line sucks, no one's going to open your email. If nobody opens your email, nobody reads it. If nobody reads it, you don't make any money. It's that simple.

So work on your subject line! The best subject lines I've found are short, concise, and often phrased in the form of a question.

Let's look at my buddy Stew with the PT testing examples:

- *Worried about failing your next PT test?*
- *Failed your last Pt test?*
- *PT test coming up?*

These subject lines will get the right people to open up the email and frankly, will not interest people who won't buy anyway.

161

Once they open your email teaser, make sure to acknowledge them rather than making them feel like this is an email a million other people are getting too. That's why I like to make sure I'm using an email software program where I can use the person's first name and fill it in, so the email starts with "Hey, Craig. Hey, Bob. Hey, Mary."

If I can't do that, then I put in something like, "Hey everyone," or "Hi Fellow Funnel Hacker," or something like that. Make people feel like they're part of the group and being acknowledged. You always need to have some salutation to start it off. Don't just dive right in.

Then you want to hit them with a shocking statement. There it is again, something to pop the reader out of their hypnosis. Something like:

Hey Craig,

- *Got a great new video for you*
- *Got an exciting new announcement*
- *Got something that's going to blow your mind*
- *Cool new, free webinar on (fantastic topic)*

You can also ask a question to start your teaser and shock them out of hypnosis.

- *Did you know that most people who try and write a book fail?*
- *What happens if you fail your next PT test?*
- *Did you know that 99 out of a 100 people who try to write a book fail?*

Once you have their attention, hit them with three or four bullets to arouse curiosity. Then tell them to click the link.

Example:

> *Subject: Want to be a published author?*
>
> *Hey Craig,*
>
> *Did you know that 99 out of a 100 people who try to write a book fail?*
>
> *Yep. It sucks. The main reasons why they fail are:*
>
> - *They don't know how to create content that sells.*
>
> - *They don't know how to get it formatted.*
>
> - *They don't know how to publish it.*
>
> *The cool news is I have a great new video that shows you exactly how to solve all those problems—**fast** and easy!*
>
> *Click here right now to see it.*
>
> *LINK*
>
> *I'll see you over there.*
>
> *Thanks,*
>
> *Jim*

That's it.

Remember: In 99 out of 100 emails, the only purpose is to get them to click a link.

One of the most successful email teasers I ever sent to my own list of prospects was only a few lines.

Subject: This blew me away

Hey Craig,

This was totally unexpected.

Somebody just did a review and it's amazing!

You've got to check this out.

LINK

See you over there,

Jim

That was the whole email. It sent the reader to a review someone did on a product of mine. That was it, and people were swept up in the curiosity of it. You have to be careful with this, so you don't appear misleading. Obviously, you wouldn't use this type of thing with people who don't know who you are (again, that email above was sent to my own in-house list).

A great email teaser breaks down like this:

- Great subject line
- Salutation
- Shocking statement
- Two, three, or four bullets or 2-4 sentences to build curiosity
- Specific call to action for what you want them to do
- Close with a personal note like "Hey, I'll see you over there. Thanks, Jim."

That's it.
Can you do it a bunch of different ways? Yes.

Is what I just outlined for you the shortcut way to do it? Absolutely, and it's going make your life a lot easier if you keep it concise. If you must err on the side of one or the other, go with a shorter email as opposed to a longer one.

Remember, you're pumping up the benefits of what they will see, *not* of what you're selling.

Just like an e-mail teaser should be short, this is a quick secret with all you need to remember:

- Get their attention to get them to open the email

- Acknowledge them

- Use a shocking statement

- Provide two, three, or four bullets to build up curiosity

- Give a specific call to action

- Close with "I'll see you over there" and your name

That's it, and it works in virtually any situation.

When you consider that 40 - 60% and more of your readers might see this message on a mobile device, this is even more important. They don't want to read a ton of text. But if they can get the basic idea and you get them excited or curious, they'll click over to check out your sales letter, video, or whatever it is.

Keep it short and sweet.

Here's one final thought about email. Email is a personal way to communicate because it arrives in their inbox. Therefore, they feel like they know you. So the more you talk to them in the quick, familiar language of a friend, the better your results.

Remember: Friends don't send friends ten-page sales letters in email!

Summary:

- 99 times out of 100 the only purpose of your email is to get a click from the right person.

- Keep it short, concise, and aimed at getting the click.

- Grab their attention and build their curiosity to entice them to click.

- Though you may send that email to a million people, remember this: they will read it one person at a time.

- Write like you're emailing a friend or colleague.

Secret #19

The Hardest Draft You'll Ever Write

"There is a secret every professional artist knows that the amateurs don't: being original is overrated. The most creative minds in the world are not especially creative; they're just better at rearrangement."
Jeff Goins

O f course, the hardest draft is the first draft. There's never a perfect time to write copy. There's always something you'd probably rather be doing. Often, when you sit down to write copy, you tell yourself you need it in the next ten minutes. So, you sit down at the computer, turn it on, open your word processor, and stare at the blinking cursor. Blink. Blink. Blink. Blink.

You think, "How in the world am I going to go from this blank screen to a sales message, a headline, a sales letter, or a video sales letter script? How in the world am I going to do that?"

The answer is to think and write in chunks. Going back to Secret #17, a sales letter is nothing more than a series of pieces. Don't think, "Hey, I have to write a sales letter." Instead, think through the chunks needed to create whatever it is you need.

In the case of a sales letter, first you need a headline. Then you need a couple of bullets followed by an introduction. Then you do the *Problem, Agitate, Solve* formula. Next, write a description of your product followed by some bullets explaining the benefits. Next, tell them a little bit about yourself. Now, provide the proof that what you're telling them works. What bonuses can you add to sweeten the pot? Next, build up the value, name the price, and then give a price drop. Now clearly state your call to action. It's time now to summarize your fantastic offer and conclude the letter. Don't forget the P.S. where you briefly restate everything and send them back to the call to action.

Yes, that's a bunch of parts, but when you think about it as parts instead of as a giant whole, then it's more manageable.

An email also has chunks. They are a subject line, salutation, *Problem, Agitate, Solve* formula with the actual solution waiting on the other side of clicking the link in the email.

A video sales letter is nothing but a series of chunks. It's your grabber on the front, a *Problem, Agitate, Solve* formula, the solution, five cool bullets about the solution, three reasons to act now, and a call to action.

The hardest draft you'll write is the first draft. That's why you want to use your swipe file to stimulate yourself and your creativity. Your swipe file provides models for copy that works. Don't look at a blank sheet. See how you can adapt sales letters you've written before, sales letters other people have written, headlines other people have written, bullets other people have written, and calls to action other people have written.

Use your swipe file to get your mind going. The first draft is why we invented www.FunnelScripts.com. With Funnel Scripts all you do is fill out an online form, whack a button and then copy and paste. It takes away the "blinking cursor" on a blank page and makes writing sales copy as easy as answering some questions. Once you get something down on paper, it's a hundred times easier to edit and rewrite than it is to write from scratch. Once you see it on paper or your screen, your mind puts it all together and says, "I should say this; I shouldn't say that. Let's move this here and that there. Oh, we need to have a guarantee. Oh, we should show a picture here. Oops, we need to have this here and that there."

Remember that all sales copy jobs are combinations of building blocks or chunks. A sales letter is a headline package, your sales story, some bullets, a guarantee, and your call to action. Are there other little parts in there? Of course, but if you think about these main building blocks, it takes away the anxiety of writing a big sales letter.

Your number one job when creating a piece of sales copy is to get the first draft or version done as fast as you can. That is the key to your success.

Summary:

- Get the first draft done as fast as you can.

- Use your swipe file to help you get it done instead of creating from scratch.

- Once you have the first draft it's a hundred times easier to edit than it is to write.

Secret #20
Make 'Em More Thirsty

*"Decide the effect you want to produce
in your reader."*
Robert Collier

Y ou've probably heard the saying, "You can lead a horse to water, but you can't make him drink." That is true. In fact, you can take a Chihuahua outside to go potty, but you can't make her pee. You can bring someone to a specific point to do what you want them to do, but you can't force them to do it. However, you can make that person more "thirsty" for what you're selling.

So the question becomes "How can I create content that makes people want to buy without giving away so much they don't need to buy?" For people who sell digital products and services, this is important. In fact, it is essential for anybody who sells anything. What you need to do is get people positioned to buy from you, but you also need to make them more "thirsty" so they buy faster.

Here is a distinction you have probably never heard before.

You've most likely heard the saying "stories sell." However, I've found stories make people "thirsty", but sales copy tells them where to buy a drink. Now I want you to think about that for just a second.

Stories make people "thirsty". Then your sales copy tells them where to go to buy a drink.

There are four different types of stories you tell people.

When we're thinking about content for your blog or social media and sales copy stories you use on a sales letter or in a video, there is no difference between them. It is your intention that makes the difference.

First, stories can be actual stories you tell about your life, your business, other people, or anything that illustrates your point.

Second, stories can be case studies, which are stories about how somebody got a result. It has a beginning, middle, and end. For instance: I was here, I wasn't happy, this is what I did with the product and these are the results I got. It's a three act play. It's just like the hero's journey.

I was here, I had a problem, this fixed it and this is where my life is now.

Third, examples can be stories as well. This is showing people how something works, how something was applied, how something was put into motion, and then the results they got.

Fourth, you can use what I call *The Three M's of Content*, which are pure gold that could potentially change your life. People are always looking for ways to give valuable content that doesn't completely solve a problem, yet creates the need for what you are selling and increases the urgency to buy right now.

The first **M** stands for dispelling a **myth**. People believe many myths. You can create massive amounts of content, such as blog posts, articles, videos, and entire webinars. In fact, whole books are written around myths people believe and the debunking of those myths.

The second **M** stands for **misconception**. Myths are basically untruths people believe, whereas misconceptions involve incorrect ideas about something. You can clear up misconceptions—including false beliefs—and replace them with correct views and clear understanding.

The third **M** stands for **mistakes**. Mistakes are where you point out where other people are going wrong. Mistakes are the most powerful of the three because nobody wants to make a mistake. Since we were little kids, we've believed if you make a mistake you're going to get a bad grade on your paper, you're going to lose a point on your test, or you're going to feel stupid. No adult wants to look stupid, so they will do anything to avoid mistakes.

You can create stories around myths, misconceptions, and mistakes, without providing any solution that is part of your product. However, when you create stories with the *Three M's of Content*, people will feel like you have been spilling the beans all day long.

And, as a bonus for you (I said there were 4 stories you can tell), there's actually a fifth way to make people even more "thirsty" using stories created from what's called "future pacing." These types of stories explain what life will be like when they take specific actions. You explain how your product, service, software—whatever—will help them achieve those results. You paint the picture by telling the story of their life when they do this.

Here's an example:

"I want you to imagine having your own unique book with your name on it as the author. You hold that book up. You show it to people. They leaf through the pages. They see your name on the front as the author. It has the same quality cover design as any New York Times bestseller. Now, imagine handing that book to someone you're trying to get to hire you to provide a service. During a job interview, you include a copy of your book with your resume. You are at a trade show handing out autographed copies of your book while everybody else hands out business cards. Think about what your life would be like when you have your own book to give out to people. How will this boost your credibility? What will your business look like? How will you feel about yourself? Obviously, having your own book is something that's important and valuable to you and your business."

What have I done there? I told a story which could be used as a Facebook post, a blog post, or even a live video. There are pictures, emotions, and all kinds of things in this story. But I haven't actually taught you how to write a book. I haven't done anything other than just make you "thirsty" to create your own book, if you haven't already, or create your next book.

Think about teaching versus selling. Teaching is stories and content. Selling is sales copy. You can use one to set up the other, and you can use them together. You can use stories in your sales letter to make people "thirsty". You can use them in your blog posts, in your videos, in your webinars. However, you need to understand the stories and content are what make people "thirsty". The selling is what shows them where to buy a drink.

Let's discuss the four ways you can sell when you're creating content (free or paid).

The first way is to give something valuable for free that naturally leads to an additional purchase. I heard a sales story years ago about a guy who runs a newspaper ad that says, "Free boat to good home." I doubt it is a true story, but maybe it is. Instantly, somebody shows up at 8:00 on Saturday morning. The guy shows him the boat and confirms, "Yep, it's free. You just have to haul it off." The buyer says, "Okay, I'll take it." Then the seller says, "One more thing. I've got a trailer over here the boat will fit on if you'd like to have it. I'll sell you the trailer, and I've also got this outboard motor over here that I'll sell you if you'd like to have an outboard motor for the boat." Whoa, think about that for a second. They're still getting a free boat, but to use it, they need a trailer to transport it and a motor to drive it.

You can give something for free. Your client will love it, but you do it in such a way that sets up the need for what you're selling. Let me give you another example. John Childers, a top-notch sales trainer, tells everybody he is a speaking coach. What he teaches is the most expensive speaker training in the world. When I went through it, it was $25,000. John sells his course in this way. You paid him $5,000 up front, attended his training, and then you agreed to give him 50% of your earned speaking fees until you have paid him another twenty thousand dollars. That was the deal.

John was an excellent trainer. This principle came home to me when John trained because his whole speaker training was about how to make money from your speaking gigs. He taught an excellent free training on how to create a high-dollar product you would sell from the back of the room at your speaking gigs. He showed you how to organize your own program. He explained in explicit detail the type of microphone you needed, how to set it up, how to use it. He described the software required to record your product. He showed you how much money you could make selling your own product from the back of the room. He was very specific about how to create the product you were going to sell from the stage to make all your money.

He gave real content. However, to sell the product you're going to create with everything he taught, you needed his speaker training to learn how to give a speech that would sell your product. He made you "thirsty" by teaching you something great that required you to buy the next step so you could put it into action.

What if you want to be a horse rider or a cowboy? Great! Let me give you free riding lessons and a free saddle and bridle. Now, let me sell you a horse.

Basically, you teach somebody something or provide something that automatically creates the need for what you're selling. But what you're giving away is so valuable and good that people don't think, "Oh, this was just a come on for them to sell me something." Instead, they think, "Damn, that's good. I want to do that. The next logical thing is to buy what they're selling so I can use what I just got here."

The second way is to tell them what to do, why they should do it, and then sell them how/what they need to do it. An example is how to write a book. I created a webinar training that details the steps to write a book:

Step one: Define your target audience.

Step two: Understand you can "create" your book's contents faster than writing it.

Step three: You're going to create that content via a phone interview.

Step four: You're going to create the cover using a designer on Fiverr. Here's the link.

Step five: You have your phone interview transcribed.

Step six: You do a light edit.

Step seven: You contract somebody on Fiverr to format your book.

Step eight: You publish it on CreateSpace (print) and Amazon Kindle (ebook).

Those are the exact steps you need to write a book.

Now, this is why you want to write a book, and all the ways it can help you.

- It gives you credibility. It gives you authority.

- You can use it as a business card when you're meeting people at trade shows.

- You can use it as a self-liquidating offer.

- You can use it as the front end of a funnel.

- You can use it to get more consulting clients, to get more speaking clients, to get more of anything.

Now that you know the steps, either you can do it manually, or you can save time by using the software that does all the steps for you. It's called *The 3-Hour Kindle Book Wizard*.

What did I do? I told you all the steps necessary to write a book SUPER fast. I can teach those steps for about 45-minutes on a webinar, which I have done dozens of times. At the end of the training, you will want to buy the software that does the whole process step-by-step for you.

The third way is to teach all the steps leading up to what you want them to purchase. For example, teach them how to set up a sales funnel for books, software, services, or coaching. Your content would include all the exact tools, pages, structure, and two weeks free use of your program. The only thing the customer has to do is write the copy for those pages. Then you tell them about a tool you have called *Funnel Scripts* which provides templates they can adapt for their sales copy, no matter what they are selling.

Or, suppose you sell a weight loss supplement that tastes like cake. You can show people different yummy recipes for how to use that weight loss supplement to create amazing, low-calorie snacks, smoothies, cookies, and other goodies. You could even do the demonstrations using video on social media targeting people in your niche audience. They see you make the recipes, they literally get hungry or thirsty watching you make the goodies, and they go buy your supplement.

The fourth way to make them "thirsty" with content is to teach them the manual or hard way to do something. Then sell them the tools, or the easy button, to do it for them. This one works so well it is almost like cheating. It is like showing somebody how to dig a well with a shovel and a ladder. You teach every single step necessary to hit the water table. At the end, you say, "Congratulations! You are fully capable of digging a well. If you don't mind, I'd like to take five minutes to tell you about this thing we have called a backhoe. It can scoop out three cubic yards of dirt at a time. Instead of digging this well over the course of a week or two by hand, and risk serious injury or death with the thing collapsing in on you, I can show you how you can dig it in about two hours using this cool tool. Would you like to see it?"

Another example would be how to build a website using HTML or CSS. You would teach how to hand code the entire website. You'd give great detail about how to do header tags, paragraph tags, line breaks, underline, bold, and italics using a free HTML editor. Then you would ask them if they would like to let *ClickFunnels* do it all for them? "And, by the way, you can automatically integrate with an autoresponder, a payment processor, up-sells, and everything else you need to do. Also, in the time it takes you to code one page by hand in a text editor, you can create your entire funnel, and be running traffic to it to see if it makes sales or not."

The bottom line with these methods is you can give away a ton of content if you structure it correctly, and make people even more thirsty for what you're selling.

Summary:

- There's no difference between the stories you use in content marketing and in your actual sales letters and sales videos.

- If you structure it right, you can give away a TON of content without giving away anything that would prevent people from buying from you.

- Remember: Stories make people "thirsty" and sales copy tells them where to go and how to buy a drink.

Secret #21

Love Me; Hate Me. There's No Money In The Middle

This secret is a fun one because this is where you purposefully create your persona or personality. People buy from a character or a persona more easily than they buy from some unknown company. That's why nameless companies or companies with big names often have spokespeople. Why? Because you can't really have a relationship with a company, or with a logo, but you can have a perceived relationship, or at least feel a certain way about a person. Everything from Ronald McDonald to Tom Bodett—"We'll leave the light on for you at Motel 6"—to the little lady with Wendy's who said, "Where's the beef?" People buy more easily from a personality or a persona.

The fastest way to establish that persona is to take a stand, to have a position or an opinion, and you need to be secure about it. That's really where the saying "Love me; hate me. There's no money in the middle." came from. Who knows who said it first? But the people in the middle don't make any money. They are so busy trying to appease everybody that they never do anything noteworthy for any particular group. If you look at politics in the United States, we have a two-party system and have for a couple of hundred years. The names of those parties have changed a few times, and the positioning of those parties has flip-flopped a couple of times, but it's an us versus them mentality. That's how people think.

It's not right or wrong; it's just the way it is. You're either with them or with us. The objective here is to pull people close to you (love me). If you force people to decide about you, some will hate you for whatever reason. They hate the tone of your voice, the cut of your suit, the fact that you're too fat, too fit, too tall, too short. They don't like your mustache. Whatever the reason, the people who hate you will still pay attention and buy from you. That's the weirdest thing of all.

I have people who hate my guts who buy from me consistently. They don't know me personally, but they hate me and still buy from me. They love to hate me. They buy my stuff to tear it apart to feel better that they don't like me. Just like the people who buy my stuff who love me. They buy my stuff, pay for my services, pay to go on cruises with me, and belong to my monthly coaching because they love me and want to feel close to me.

You can do the same thing. But, to get results, you must force people to decide about you. You do this in your content and sales copy. You do it by taking a position and being consistent with your message, your methods, your opinions, who you like, and who you don't. Even though you don't talk smack about people by name, you can talk about behavior. You can discuss practices. You can talk about methods.

You need to have a position. "This is right; this is wrong. This is good; this is bad. This works; this doesn't work." People are looking for a leader, for someone to blaze the trail for them. They want someone to tell them, "This will burn your hand, little Johnny. Don't put your freaking hand on the stove." Or, "Hey Sally, this little bunny rabbit is soft and fluffy and will make you feel wonderful if you pet it." They're looking for someone to tell them their version of the truth, to give them the right story, to guide them, and to be consistent about it. That's why customers get so irritated with people that have the newest, greatest thing of the week and why those types of marketers, or sellers, or promoters have to spend more time trying to replenish their list than they should because they're always coming out with the next greatest thing. *You need to be consistent.* However, don't be afraid to change direction. If the world changes, if circumstances change, if something makes you re-evaluate your opinion, then you need to tell people, "Hey, I've changed my opinion about this. I've changed my practice." But don't be wishy-washy. Don't be like the wave on the ocean getting tossed around. You need to stand firm.

Look at this quick example: For many years we did article marketing which was our primary way to drive traffic to our website. Every week I created an article and promoted it using a service called *Submit Your Article*. It posted your article in different announcement sites on the web, which drove thousands of visitors a week to my websites. At the time, it was the only thing I taught to get traffic.

One day, it stopped working. Google changed its algorithms. They stopped counting all those articles because people did spammy articles of little or no value. All that traffic through Google dried up, literally overnight. Instead of trying to milk it and tell people, "Well, it may come back," I said, "You know what? This process isn't working anymore, so we need to figure out something else."

You can't be afraid to change direction.

I heard this saying, "Love me; hate me. There's no money in the middle," from Matt Furey at a mastermind meeting in Tampa Florida in February of 2003. When Matt spoke to the group, he looked at me and said, "I just bought your book, and you're selling it way too cheap." My eyes got wide because this is a pretty impressive guy.

I thought, "This guy forces you to form an opinion about him."

Then he said, "The other thing that's made a big difference in my business is operating with the philosophy, "Love me; hate me. There's no money in the middle."

It floored me. I'll never forget hearing that for the first time. It's made a dramatic impact on my business because this philosophy gave me the courage to stand up to people who were saying things that weren't true. This philosophy gave me the courage to change direction. It gave me the courage to share my opinion. Because of this philosophy, I know that if I try to please everybody all the time, nothing good will come from it.

When it comes to your copy and content, always remember, "Love me; hate me. There's no money in the middle." Have a strong opinion. Stick with your opinion. Don't be afraid to change if the world proves you need to change. Be a consistent character for the people who pay attention to you.

Summary:

- Love me; hate me. There's no money in the middle.
- Stand for something!
- Be consistent in your message, opinion, and what you stand for.
- Don't be afraid to change direction and explain why to people if the situation warrants it.

Secret #22

"Oh Damn—I Got To Have That!"

"It has long been my belief that a lot of money can be made by making offers to people who are at an emotional turning point in their lives."
Gary Halbert

The number one key to selling like crazy is the promise any profitable product makes. Whatever sales copy you're assembling, 99 percent of the time your headline is your number one most important component. The promise of any product or service, often contained in that headline, is the number one key to selling like crazy.

As with any sales copy, there's a formula for creating a profitable promise. In this case it's a four-part formula. They are 1) the hurdle, 2) the prize, 3) the timing, and 4) the eliminator. Let's take a look at each of them.

Part One: The Hurdle

First, you must address people's concerns or questions about what they have to do to get what they want. When someone looks at your product, while you tell them, "Hey, this will help you get the result you want," they think, "Okay, but what do I have to do to *get* that result?" Your job is to understand the thing they want but see as a hard thing to do, which is the hurdle. The result is the thing they see on the other side. It's where they get what they want. To understand their obstacle, pay close attention to the action words they use. 99% of the time, the hurdle is some action that needs to get taken.

Whatever action keywords your target audience uses are significant. You need to pay attention to the differences, like "how to drive a golf ball" versus "how to hit a golf ball" versus "how to strike a golf ball". Or "how to meet beautiful women" versus "how to date beautiful women" versus "how to find beautiful women". Do you see the hurdle, the action? The ability to take the action to get the result is what they see holding them back. This action creates a mental image. People visualize actions best because they involve motion, and 80 percent of your brain focuses on handling what you see. Secondly, you process motion most with your optical hardware whether you imagine it internally or see it externally. That's why, when you see movement out of the corner of your eye, you turn your head. You're wired up to do that.

Therefore, we want to give people mental images to literally and figuratively turn their head inside their mind. So: "How to do or accomplish something." It's something they want done for them. So how to **get**, how to **have**, how to **claim**, how to **write**, how to **publish**, how to **create**, how to **use**, or how to **access**. What do they want to do? What is the action or the verb they desire? "How to lose 20 pounds. How to paint your house. How to train your dog. How to teach your kid to lift the toilet seat." The actions are the hurdles.

Part Two: The Prize

The prize is what the person wants. It is also known as the result you want from the taking action in the previous step. For example:

- You want your own outrageously profitable e-book and fat royalty checks
- You want a passionate relationship
- You want freedom from back pain
- You want to golf like a seasoned pro

Again, pay close attention to the result keywords your niche uses. Some examples:

- How to drive a golf ball like Tiger Woods
- How to hit a golf ball like Arnold Palmer
- How to strike a golf ball like a veteran PGA pro

For some audiences, they know who Arnold Palmer is but they're more familiar with Tiger Woods or Sam Snead. You need to understand the words they use for the prize when you start crafting and using the formula to create your profitable product promises.

Part Three: The Timing

Answer the question *When will I get what I want?* Basically, many of us are highly-functioning five-year-olds, wondering when Santa Claus will show up and give us what we want. So even though you're an adult, your inner youth is screaming, "Well, when will I get it? When will it show up? How long do I have to wait? I want it now!"

The timing part of the formula is where you give a timeframe they can wrap their head around that answers their question *When will I get it?* Will it be an hour, an afternoon, a day, a weekend, or a week? How long will it take? There are two ways to present timing. First, you reference the time it takes for them to get the prize by taking action themselves. The key is that it should be almost unbelievable, but within the realm of possibility so they can only blame themselves if they don't do it.
Examples:

- Timing: Write a 100-page book in about a week.

  o To write a hundred page e-book in seven days is very possible. It can be done in two to three days if you sit down and do it. But if you don't do it, then you know you didn't do the work.

- Timing: Create a real Kindle book in 90 minutes.

  o To create a nice little Kindle book in 90-minutes is very possible with technology and strategy, if you know what you're doing.

The second way to present time is saying how long it takes you to teach them how to get the prize. For example:

A. How to improve your golf swing in two 30-minute sessions

B. How to improve your English in one hour

C. Give me 17-minutes, and I'll show you how to start a conversation with the most beautiful woman in the room

The timing can be either how long it takes for them to do it, or how long it takes you to teach them.

Part Four: The Eliminator

The eliminator lets them off the hook, as in "it's not their fault" they don't have what they want yet. Everyone puts up mental barriers about what's stopping them, such as stumbling blocks, or obstacles, or painful actions, or they don't know the next step, or other perceived barriers holding them back. Whether they're real or imagined, these are real barriers to them. It's going to take too long, cost too much, be too hard, or they don't know what to do. If you don't eliminate the excuse that holds them back, then you're screwed.

The excuses result from past effort, pain, or failure. It may well be their fault for not getting the results they want, but you can't tell them it's their fault because they'll get all pissy and defensive. Remember that you **never** say it's their fault. Let me repeat that. **Under no circumstances do you tell them it is their fault for not getting the results they want.** Yeah, I know the reason many people can't lose weight is because they don't have enough sense to push back from the table before they eat that third cheeseburger. But I won't tell them that. I will tell them, "It's not your fault because you've been lied to about how carbs and proteins and vegetables interact. And if you will just change your strategy for how you eat, you will start losing weight." When it comes to sales copy, it's not their fault. Ever. Burn that into your brain.

This last part of the formula forces you to make a better offer. You have to remove what's holding the person back in order to get the sale. And when you remove what's holding them back, your offer will be incredible because this formula forces you to think creatively.

Let's look at a quick example that starts to pull it all together: "How to write and publish your own outrageously profitable e-book in as little as seven days." That has three of the parts, but no eliminator. The reader says, "Oh, that's awesome. But I'm not a writer, so this won't work for me."

So we add this little bit at the end: ". . . even if you can't write, can't type, and failed high school English class." That's your eliminator. Notice the use of the transition "even if," or "even if you can't" to let them off the hook. Or you can add the phrase "without _____" and you have, "How to write and publish your own outrageously profitable eBook in as little as seven days without typing a single word of it yourself."

So, whatever the pain, whatever the effort, whatever tough actions they'd expect, you want to sweep those out from under them, so they say, "Oh, dang. You mean I don't have to sit there and type it? You mean I don't have to sit there and write it? You mean I don't have slave away at the keyboard? Okay, you got my attention!"

There are some promise superchargers you can add to make this formula even more powerful. The first is the money promise, but be careful with this one. "Make as much as an extra hundred dollars a day." "How to make a thousand dollars as a _____ or with _____ or doing _____." And you can forgive past mistakes. "Even if you've tried before and failed." "How to write and publish your own outrageously profitable e-book in as little as seven days, even if you've tried to publish a book before and failed miserably." Or "Even if you hate writing and can only type with two fingers."

The second is with a timeline or with timing. "In 60 minutes or less;" "In seven days or less;" "in less than a week;" or "in less than an hour."

The third is a cost modifier. "For less than $50;" "For less than the cost of a cup of coffee at Starbucks;" "For less than a medium everything pizza every month." Use this supercharger in such a way that they think, "Oh damn. So, for less than it costs to get a medium pizza every month, I can have this? Heck, yeah."

Now, in what niche groups of people does this formula work? It works with everyone who needs a problem solved or has an intense desire. You don't have to use these elements in order, but you want to try to put them in your titles, headlines, and promises. The biggest thing you need to know is what they want or what's their number one problem.

Let's look at some examples.

1. Dating: "How to use online dating sites like match. com to find the love of your life in 30 days without wasting time on the wrong people." "How to use online dating sites like match.com to find the love of your life within 30 days and it costs less than an everything pizza to join." "How to use online dating sites like match.com to find the love of your life within 30 days, even if you've failed at online dating before."

2. Real estate: "How you can use eBay Real Estate to cash in with your first money-making deal within 72-hours, no matter where you live in the world. All you need is internet access and a desire to make money." "How you can use eBay Real Estate to cash in on your first money-making deal within 72-hours, even if you've never bought a house before in your life." "How you can use eBay Real Estate to cash in on your first money-making deal within 72-hours, even if you have no money of your own to invest."

3. Marital advice: "How to get your spouse or lover talking again and save your relationship with one

15-minute session, even if everything you've tried in the past didn't work." "How to get your spouse or lover talking again and save your relationship in one 15-minute session, even if you've experienced a failed marriage in the past."

4. Dog training: "Seven cool tricks every dog can learn in a weekend. Fun, fast, and stress-free."

The bottom line is, when you use all four parts of the Profitable Product Promise formula—the hurdle, the prize, the timing, and the eliminator—to hit the hot buttons and check all the boxes that your prospects need to buy, you create irresistible offers that address all the things that are holding them back.

Summary:

- The promise you make in your sales copy directly affects how many people buy from you.

- When you make an amazing promise (and fulfill it) your sales can go through the roof.

- Include each part of the formula because each hits a critical point in your prospects decision making process.

- Never, EVER make them feel like it's their fault they don't have what they want yet.

Secret #23

Put Lipstick On The Pig

"Nobody reads ads. People read what interests them.
Sometimes it's an ad."
Howard Gossage

How do you make bad or underperforming copy pop? Sometimes you can't, and it's easier to start over. Sometimes you'll work on something, pour your blood, sweat, and tears into it, and it just plain sucks. Sometimes it's best to walk away from it.

However, sometimes you can put lipstick on a pig and turn it into a beauty queen.

Here's what to do if your copy isn't working: ask yourself a series of questions. You want to see whether or not you've missed something that is causing one or more areas of your copy to underperform.

Look at the headline.

- Do you have a headline? You'd be surprised how many people don't have a headline. Why in the world would anybody not have a headline? It is the first thing somebody sees on your page. It can also be the first words that come out of your mouth in a video sales letter. You'd be surprised how many people don't have anything even remotely resembling a headline.

- Is your headline about you or your audience? Once I had a headline about how I went from trailer trash to piles of cash. I thought it was an amazing headline. It fell flat on its face! But when I changed it to how to gain a positively unfair advantage in business and life, then my sales took off by over 500 percent.

- Is there a big, bold benefit or promise? You can always create a headline that causes people to stop what they're doing. A great example is saying something like, "Sex!" Or, "Emergency!" The problem is that it makes the wrong people stop. So they stop and read it, and then they get pissed off because it has nothing to do with them (or sex). So is there a bold benefit or promise in your headline that's going to attract the right people to stop and pay attention?

Is the offer clear?

- Does the buyer understand what they will get? Is it crystal clear? "You're going to get this, this, this, this, this and this."

- How do they get it? Is it delivered digitally? Does it come overnight? Is it a physical product? Is it an electronic product? Is it coaching? What is it?

- When do they get it? Do they get it instantly? Do they get it tomorrow? Do they get it next week? Do they get it once a month for the next 12 months? Is it on-demand?

- How much does it cost? If they can't tell how much it is fairly easily by reading your message, you turn people off, because they feel like you're hiding something.

Is there a clear reason to buy now?

Is there a clear reason for them to buy right now? You can have the greatest offer in the world, but if there's no urgency to buy now, then they won't. Traditionally, these are the three ways to get people to buy now:

- Bonuses. Stack on added value to your fantastic offer if they buy right now.

- Time deadline. People often use this with large product launches. They set the deadline and shut down the offer on that Friday. The problem comes in when, next Tuesday, they tell you their buddy emailed them, "Hey, please can you open this up just for my people for 24 hours?" The person thought, "Well, that's not fair. So I have to open it up for everybody for 24 hours. So in case you missed it, or in case you waited, you have 24 hours again." If you do that, you just blew your integrity.

- Limited quantities. This is a double-edged sword. You have a high performing offer, but when you run out of limited quantities, that's when people see if you have any integrity. If you magically add more quantities, and the offer keeps going, the people who bought realize you lied.

When I launched my first big product about how to create your own multimedia info products, I learned a valuable lesson about time deadlines. In 2003, I was one of the first people in the world to show people how to create content and burn it to CD or deliver it over the web. It was cutting edge, with screen capture video and full motion video. I made enough money from that promotion to pay off my house.

When the time deadline came that I promised to stop selling the product, I was bummed out. My wife asked, "What's wrong?" I said, "I've got a perfect offer and a great product. And I can never sell it again." To keep my integrity, I had to respect the time deadline and never sell the product again.

I learned my lesson. When I came out with my next big product, I did not use time deadlines or limited quantities. Instead, I used the fear of losing out, which is a much better reason for them to buy now. That product ended up making around five million dollars because I wasn't stupid enough to depend on the time deadline. It takes a little more skill to come up with, but if you can incorporate the fear of losing out into your copy, then you do much better.

How do you use this technique? You use what's called *future pacing*. "Hey, if you don't buy this, here's what's going to happen: You won't be able to do this or have that. You won't have the ability to (whatever)." And if you lay on three, four, or five reasons why waiting will result in their lunch eaten by a competitor or be stuck where they are, you don't have to depend on things like time deadlines and limited quantities. You can do a lot better for a lot longer.

Fear   Desire

Curiosity   Pain

Is there an emotional driver in the copy?

Do you have an emotion to grab people right at the beginning of your copy? It can be fear, desire, curiosity, pain, pleasure, satisfaction, or dissatisfaction (when you talk about problems).

There has to be emotion infused into your copy. You create it by circumstances they either want to get rid of or want to create. Your copy either drives them towards something they want or helps them to move away from something they don't like. They're moving toward something they want or running away from something they hate. But there has to be an emotional component in the copy.

So, if your copy's not performing, you need to look at it and say, "Is there something here that grabs people emotionally other than the promise to make money?" And nine times out of ten, from my experience, people buy out of dissatisfaction with their current circumstances.

People may be driven, or at least somewhat motivated by, what they want, but what gets people to act is dissatisfaction. Because, if things are good enough, people will sit on the crappy couch, eating Cheetos, watching a TV that is sort of tuned in, because, until it hurts enough to make a change, people don't change.

So remember that. Nine times out of ten, people buy out of dissatisfaction with current circumstances. It creates the drive to buy now, rather than put it off.

Do your bullets suck?

Are your bullets curiosity drivers, or are they boring, bland, and read like a technical manual? We've done an entire secret on bullets and the proper bullet formula (see Secret #9). So the question is, are you featuring features, or are you highlighting benefits and payoffs? Bullets are what build the desire and curiosity that drive people to take action, enter their credit card information (especially online), and buy from you.

What about the price?

Is the price too high relative to what others are charging? Now, that doesn't mean you can't charge a premium price as long as your offer justifies charging a premium price. On the flip side, is your price too low, creating the perception that you're too cheap?

Think about it. For example, if you had a course on how to do options trading focused on a biz-op, work-at-home market for $97, you might do very well. You have a very different price than if you focus on a group of experienced investors looking to branch out into an options or futures market. If they saw your product was $97, they would laugh and think it wasn't even worth their time. They'd think it was way too cheap and wasn't worth anything. So your price can be too high, but it can also be too low. How do you find out? Test.

When you look at your price, ask if the value is there. Does it feel like a great deal? Does it feel like, "Wow! This offer is amazing. I need to buy this before they raise the price or change their minds."

There's a concept called selling dollars for dimes that I learned from a man named Marlon Sanders. In the prospect's mind, your offer combined with your bonuses must be worth ten times what you charge. That seems to be the magic number.

Now, whether it needs to be ten-to-one or twenty-to-one or five-to-one or thirteen-to-one isn't the issue. Your offer must feel like you're selling dollars for dimes. Think of it this way: If somebody offered, "I will sell you as many dollars as you want for just 10 cents apiece. How many do you want?" Your answer is, "As many as I can get." That's the feeling you want people to have.

If your sales price is $97, you want to give a thousand dollars in demonstrable value. That's selling dollars for dimes. If you're charging a thousand dollars, then you want somebody to feel they're getting ten thousand dollars' worth of value.

Now, like I said, it's not always ten-to-one. But it has to feel like this is a fantastic, authentic, real deal. So if your copy's not performing, it may be the price, or the perceived value, that's not where it needs to be.

Are you using the right graphics and colors?

Do your graphics add to the message? Do you have any graphics? If you do, do they raise the emotion, distract people, or make people feel bad when they look at your copy even if they don't know why?

Be careful with your colors. Do your colors match, or does it look like a psychedelic acid trip? Is the website so ugly it makes you want to smack its mama? You are better off with a site that's plain and conservative than you are with one that's crazy and assaults people's eyeballs.

You do want to use graphics appropriately. Each major point or idea in your sales copy should have an accompanying graphic.

What about proof?

It could be that people don't believe you. Do you offer proof, especially around your claims? Any time you make a claim, you need to have something to back it up. It could be a testimonial, a case study, some statistics, or an expert endorsement. Whenever people could think, "Mm, I'm not sure about that," or "I doubt that," or some smart aleck in the back of a room screams, "Prove it!" that's when you need to have some sort of third-party validation that what you're doing works and is accurate.

Your proof could be screenshots, before and after pictures with weight loss, or photographs of bank statements, checks, and closing statements. But you need to be careful that you can genuinely substantiate these kinds of authentication. The FTC loves to come after these claims.

As a side note, if you're in investing, weight loss, or anything that involves people's health or their money, you need to be doubly cautious about any claims you make and use the right disclaimers. Any pictures or testimonials you use must be 100 percent rock solid. You don't want to run into a situation where you can't substantiate it because you haven't kept good records.

These are several of the ways to put lipstick on a pig. While they aren't all the ways, they're a darn good start.

Summary:

- If your copy is not performing, try putting some lipstick on it. That means going through this list to ensure you haven't missed anything.

- #1 thing to test is your headline (assuming you have one) to see how that affects conversion.

- Make sure your offer is very clear and they know what they're getting.

- Try selling dollars to dimes to see if you can improve the performance of your copy.

Secret #24

Should I Join The Dark Side?

"Copy cannot create desire for a product. It can only take the hopes, dreams, fears and desires that already exists in the hearts of millions of people, and focus those already existing desires onto a particular product. This is the copy writer's task: not to create this mass desire—but to channel and direct it."

Eugene Schwartz

There are two ways you can go negative with your copywriting. There's one good way and one bad way. The good way to go negative is to meet people in their internal conversation. You talk about their problems, their mistakes, their fears, and their enemies (real or perceived). You warn against adverse events and advice. Use the negative going on inside of their head to get in sync with them. Because until you get in sync with them, they won't pay attention to you.

Let's look at a couple of examples. What problems would dog trainers have? Perhaps getting more clients. A negative could be, "Are you having trouble attracting good clients for your dog training business?" "Are you dealing with problem customers?" You lead with a negative like this.

How about real estate investors? What negative could you lead with? "Having trouble finding good deals?" "Having trouble with no money for down payment?" "Do you have bad credit?" "Is bad credit holding you back from finding or financing your deals?" "Can you find deals, but you can't find any way to fund them?" These are all negatives you can use to enter the conversation going on in somebody's mind.

How about doctors? "Has malpractice insurance crushed your profitability?" Whoa, now that's something to think about. Maybe a doctor has staffing problems. Maybe a doctor has issues with patient satisfaction. "Have a problem with health insurance not paying out on time or cutting your fees?"

How about funnel hackers? "Can't get enough traffic?" "Ads not converting?" "Trouble getting all the mechanics set up for your funnels?"

Use the negative to get in sync with somebody. Once you get in sync with them, then you transition to your solution. Nobody cares about your answer until they know you care about their problem. There's an adage that says, "Nobody cares how much you know until they know how much you care." You may think that's an old, tired, worn out phrase, but it is as valid now as it has ever been. Especially with online sales copy.

So once they know you're paying attention to them because you acknowledged their problem, then you demonstrate the solution to the problem. You explain how your product prevents mistakes. You put their fears to rest with proof. You show how to defeat their enemies. Whether they're real or perceived, those enemies are real to them, and that's all that matters. Then you give them a roadmap or inoculate them against future adverse events.

Those are all excellent negatives to include in your copywriting, content, and communication. They are like public service announcements. You can think about it this way, "I'm helping you avoid problems. I'm helping you overcome roadblocks. I'm answering the questions that are holding you back." You are performing a public service for your target audience, whether it's through your copywriting, videos, or content.

So that's the good way to go negative. Use the bad to get in sync with where your potential customer is right now.

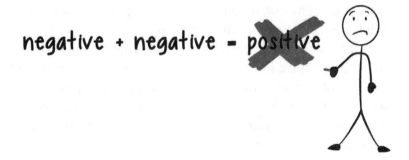

negative + negative - positive

Let's look at the negative negatives. And by the way, a negative negative does not make a positive. The best example of what not to do is any political attack ad you've ever seen. These ads that call names and throw dirt create a toxic environment for everyone. You might think, "I would never do that in my business." That's wonderful. But I have seen people do this, and it is detrimental.

Bottom line: you never outright attack somebody. You can attack behavior. If you see something that somebody's doing, say, "You know what? I've seen people doing this, and I don't think it's right. Here is why and what people should do instead." You can attack results if they don't make sense or could ultimately hurt them. For example, a chiropractor sees somebody teach a patient to do a particular exercise that would injure somebody. Then you should bring that to people's attention.

You can also attack a method. "Why would you keep doing things the way they did them in the last century when we've had advances in technology and strategy that make it a hundred times easier to get results? So stop doing things the old way; start doing things the new way."

You can attack behavior. You can attack results. You can attack a method. But you never attack a person or a company by name. You never, ever call somebody out. It never pays off. It only creates problems. And it will come back and bite you ninety-nine times out of a hundred.

Now, here's what we don't mean by not going negative. That sounds like a triple negative. We don't mean that everything is super positive. There's a Disney character named Pollyanna who was positive about everything. She would, no matter what anyone said, find the positive spin on it. She was so sickly sweet, I wanted to reach through the screen and choke her. This girl fell out of a third-story window, broke her back, and was still positive about everything as they carried her away at the end of the movie. So we don't want to fall into that trap of "everything's always positive." That won't resonate with people.

What if you are in a situation where you must compare and contrast yourself with someone else? Especially if somebody is doing something that is not in people's best interest? You want to say something like this, "Now some of our competitors will tell you _____, but that's just not true. Here are the facts you need to know." You don't mention anybody by name. For instance, "Some of our competitors will tell you it's okay to use a choke chain when training a large dog, but that's not true. Here are the facts you need to know." "Some of our competitors will tell you to use a third-party email service provider to send your email, but that's not a good idea. Here are the facts that you need to know." "Some of our competitors will tell you they have great deliverability rates just like us, but that's not true. Here are the facts you need to see."

This is a way you can sweep the legs out from under them. Without mentioning anyone by name or calling them out, you say, "You know, this is not true." Or you can say something like, "You may have noticed some people are

_____, but we don't think that's right. Here's why." "You may have noticed some people charge extra for _____, but we don't think that's right. Here's why." "You may have noticed some people make you pay for a separate third-party email relay service, but we don't think that's right. Here's why." You're getting the message out there, but you're sweeping it out of the way and saying what you think is essential for them to make a good decision (which is to buy from you).

Whatever your target audience has experienced, you can key in on a negative without being confrontational or combative or attacking someone by name.

Remember, you can go negative without joining the dark side by using the negative to get in sync with people. You can always attack the behavior, the idea, or practice, but never, ever name names.

Summary:

- There's a good way and a bad way to "go negative."

- Use negatives to get in sync with people and the conversations going on in their heads.

- Never go negative by attacking someone or a company by name. It never pays off and very often backfires.

Secret #25

"Stealth" Closes—The Secret To Selling Without Selling

"Tap a single overwhelming desire existing in the hearts of thousands of people who are actively seeking to satisfy it at this very moment."
Eugene Schwartz

Wouldn't it be amazing to turn any piece of content, any video, any article, any blurb, snippet, or even the humblest tweet into your secret sales agent any time you want? Of course it would. Is it possible to sell without selling? How do you put sales into content like info videos, articles, and stuff that's not sales-oriented? The answer is Stealth Closes (aka The Columbo Close).

In the TV show *Columbo*, the main character was a police detective who investigated murders or heinous crimes. Because he appeared humble and bumbling, nobody took him seriously. The bad guys didn't see him as a threat but more of a nuisance. In every episode, the bad guy or gal thought they had gotten away with the crime. In the last 30 seconds to five minutes, Columbo would show up, ask a few questions, act like everything was fine, and then say, "Oh, by the way, what happened with that drink or empty cup I saw on the bar?" Or, "Whatever happened with that?" The person's guard was down, so they would answer the question which would convict them.

The Columbo Close is a way to fly under people's radar. Most people looking at advertising have their defenses up. Whether consciously or subconsciously they think, "This person is trying to sell me something. I have to be careful because every time I see one of these ads I end up buying something. Then my wife yells at me because I'm racking up the credit cards. So, I have to be careful. I'm buying nothing. I'm just looking." They have their anti-sale radar on full blast. A Stealth Close is a very subtle way to direct someone where you want them to go without them realizing what you are doing.

Often, you start a Stealth Close with these three words: "By the way." Let me show you a real example from an email teaser I sent.

Subject Line: Hey, [first name], the perfect picture.

Jim Edwards here with an article below that will get published in my newspaper column tomorrow, but you get the scoop today. So if you make websites, mini-sites, content sites, brochures, fliers, e-book covers, DVD covers, or anything else that requires images, this article has some excellent information for you that will save you both time and money.

By the way, it's still not too late to sign up for the Website Video Secrets workshop in LA next week. Get all the details here at websitevideosecrets.com."

Now, what does the Video Secrets workshop have to do with the newspaper column? Absolutely nothing. But I whack them out of the blue after I've given them value.

The Stealth Close also works well in the P.S. of a message. Here's another example:

"I've got an article for you about how people are fencing stolen goods on eBay, and you need to be careful." And then, "P.S. We have a few seats left for our live Website Video Secrets Workshop in Atlanta on April 5th and 6th. If you want to discover the secrets to making simple little videos that drive traffic, make people click, and generate fat commissions, get more information here right now."

Then I included the link. Again, it's a pivot. Think about a judo jiu-jitsu move. The person comes at you with one thing, you step to the side, and they get flipped.

So, how does this work?

There are two parts. In part one, you give some value. In the above example, I gave value. "Hey, here's a cool article. Here's a video. Here's (what-have-you)." Then in step two, you invite them to another level by merely using the words "by the way."

Where do you use a Stealth Close to get the best results? They work exceptionally well in email teasers. Often, I will send the email with the value just so that I can give the Stealth Close. It's like the value I offer is the toll I pay to deliver the Stealth Close message. This close is different from a sponsor ad or a display ad that screams, "Hey, this is an ad. You can ignore me." It's virtually impossible for them to separate the Stealth Close from the rest of the message, which is the whole purpose of it.

As an example:

> *"P.S. We have a few seats left for our live Website Video Secrets Workshop in Atlanta. If you want to discover the secrets to making simple little videos that drive traffic, make people click, and generate fat commissions, get more information here right now."*

You can use the Stealth Close technique verbally, in text, or anywhere. First you deliver value and then pivot to get a signup, a subscriber, whatever you want to get done.

You can also use this type of close in articles. At the end of a pretty long article I published, it says, "By the way, if you'd like to sell more, promote your books, and create incredible content using interviews, The Expert Interview Wizard helps you make everything you need to create and promote amazing, profitable interviews in just three to five minutes flat. Watch the demo and get a special price, but only for a limited time, interviewwizardspecial.com."

On the surface, does that appear to be an ad? No. It just pivots from content to the next step I want them to take. Also, (and this is key) it's not formatted any differently from the rest of the material. That's important. Nothing screams ad faster than something that stands out as different. It screams, "Hey, I'm not content."

You can also do this in blog posts. In a blog post all about Evergreen Products, I taught how to create them, how to make them, and why you want to have them. And then the pivot is, "By the way, one of the easiest and most useful Evergreen Info Products you can create is an interview with an expert. Either you as the expert providing information or you as the host interviewing someone else. Interviews are not only easy to create, but you can publish them as books, e-books, DVDs, webinars, teleseminars, home study courses, and more. Interviews are like the Swiss Army Knife of the info product creation world. One more thing, if you'd like to sell more, promote more . . . ." It is formatted the same as the rest of the blog post.

You can use Stealth Closes in your Kindle books. So if you're publishing Kindle books, regular books, or e-books, you can use Stealth Closes any time you mention a resource. You can even do a Stealth Close at the beginning of your book to get more subscribers, including the people that don't buy. At the beginning of that book, have a page that says, "By the way, if you'd like a free audiobook version, head on over to mysite.com/audiobook and register your copy now."

This is a great example of how you can leverage copywriting in something where people aren't expecting sales copy.

This format works in Facebook posts, YouTube videos, Pinterest, or anywhere you create and share content. This method also works well on Facebook live videos. End every video with a "by the way" statement and direct them to something that makes you money or gets you a subscriber. It's easy and effective when you get in the habit of doing it.

Why do you want to use Stealth Closes instead of the usual direct call to action?

Because the typical call to action is something like this, "Click here now to _____." There's nothing wrong with that. It works well in the right circumstances, but people also know what's coming. People know, "This is where they transition from the free stuff to selling me something. This is where they want me to sign up for something." Don't get me wrong. I've made millions of dollars with that phrase, "Click here now to _____." It has its place, especially on a sales letter or on a sales page, where someone knows they're in a sales situation.

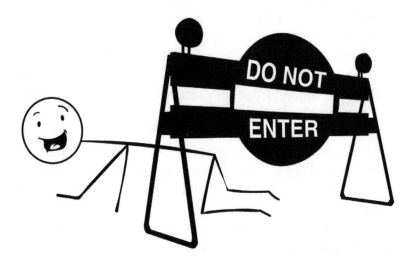

But what if they don't know they're in a sales situation? Or they don't want to be in a sales situation? Or they don't want to go from Facebook, where they're getting all this free content, over to somewhere else where you might try to sell them something? That's when the Stealth Closes come in because people's defenses are up. A Stealth Close allows you to slide in under their defenses just like a Stealth Bomber. We use Stealth Closes to drive traffic from free content to paid offers. You don't use a Stealth Close on an actual sales letter or in a video sales letter.

Let's talk about how to use Stealth Closes to drive traffic from free content to paid offers. Step one is to teach them something, to offer value. Hook them in with the promise (and delivery) of value. Give them tips. My buddy, Mike Stewart, likes to call them "Didja Knows?" So, "Didja know there are three ways to create and publish a book without writing? Absolutely. Here they are."

You solve problems. "Hey, are you having trouble figuring out how to get a great-looking cover for your Kindle books? Not a problem. I will show you right now how you can get a great-looking cover made for five dollars."

Answer questions. "Hey, have you ever wondered how I make sales of my Kindle book once I post it to Amazon? Well, you know, a lot of people have that same question. Here are five things to help you answer that question."

Then step two is to say, "By the way, did you know _____? Well, _____ and _____, it's true. Check it out." Example: "Hey, by the way, did you know that 3-Hour Kindle Book Wizard will help you create and publish your book in less than three hours of total effort? It's true. Check it out."

Or, "Hey, did you know there is a software you can fill out in about 10 minutes that will create everything you need to create and publish your book on Amazon? It's true, and you can check out a demo right here at 3-Hour Kindle Book Wizard."

Whatever you teach them, use a "by the way" statement to tell them where they can get a benefit. You tie it into an advantage they want, that goes along with whatever you taught them. The easiest way is to tie them to the ten reasons why people buy anything from Secret #3.

1. Make money

2. Save money

3. Save time

4. Avoid effort

5. Escape mental or physical pain

6. Get more comfort

7. Achieve greater cleanliness or hygiene to attain better health

8. Gain praise

9. Feel more loved

10. Increase their popularity or social status

Hopefully you see how these Copywriting Secrets play off one another and help you to get better at copywriting.

Let's make using Stealth Closes a habit because that's where you find the real profits. Use Stealth Closes a lot so you get the benefits ongoing. Here's your rule to live by. Any time you publish anything, take the words—by the way, did you know—and tell them something.

By the way, did you know that you can _____ with _____? Yep, it's true. Go here for more information.

By the way, did you know _____ will help you _____? Yep, it's true. Go here for a quick demo.

By the way, did you know we still have _____ available? Yep, it's true. Go here to find out more.

By the way, did you know _____ is on sale for _____? Yep, it's true. Go here to find out how you can grab one for 75% off.

Stealth Closes could be the most potent secret weapon in your content marketing arsenal because hardly anybody knows about them. They don't even think about it. Everyone uses that direct frontal assault as a call to action. The other reason you should use them is they work great. They fly under people's radar, and you can incorporate sales copy into everything you do without people realizing it.

Now, if you're thinking, "Well, if I say 'by the way' all the time, people will begin to recognize that and see it coming, and it will be just like any other ad." Maybe. But there other things you can say like, "Oh, before I forget;" "Oh, one more thing;" "Hey, by the way;" "Hey, did you know?" "Hey, did you realize?" There are so many different ways to make that segue and do the Stealth Close to get surprising results.

There are a million different ways to use Stealth Closes. Commit that nothing you do goes out without a close, no matter how unlikely it might be. When you do this consistently, you will see an amazing transformation in the number of people who do what you want them to do as a result of viewing your content.

Summary:

- People's sales radar defenses are up all the time.

- Stealth Closes help you fly under their defenses and get them to take the actions you want them to take.

- Make the commitment that you will include a Stealth Close somewhere in your free (and paid) content to drive people to your sales copy and offers.

Secret #26
The Hired Gun

"If you think it's expensive to hire a professional to do the job, wait until you hire an amateur."
Red Adair

ere are some realities of outsourcing sales copy. I am not a huge fan of outsourcing copy. Not because I'm a glutton for punishment and not because I think that sitting around and creating copy is the most exciting thing in the world I could be doing compared to other stuff.

But the reality is that nobody knows your product as well as you do. Nobody knows your market as well as you do. So half the problem, or the challenge, of hiring somebody to write copy for you is that you have to teach them all they need to know about your product and your market to be able to figure out how to write sales copy for you.

You can't say, "I'm going to go find somebody to write me a sales letter in my orchid growing niche. Let me go find an orchid growing copywriter." It's not that easy. To find a good copywriter, you have to find somebody who understands your product and market. 999 times out of 1,000, the only way that happens is, you have to teach them.

An outside perspective can be good sometimes, especially if you are not an experienced copywriter. If you're too close to your product, an outside person can help you see the forest for the trees as opposed to being focused on one tree.

However, I've found that if you're looking for an outside perspective, it's more helpful to hire a good, experienced copywriter to critique your copy once you've created it. Ask them to do something similar to Secret #23: Putting Lipstick on the Pig. They can run down the checklist to see where there's a problem.

To have somebody write copy for you, they're going to ask you lots and lots of questions. You will do at least one big, extended interview with them, if not more, which is a lot of work. You have to sit down and identify your market, what are the benefits, what are the payoffs, what is your audience's motivation, what is the emotional impact, what is their reason to buy, how to get them to buy now, and what the limited time bonus is, etc.

Then you must communicate all that information to someone else who is unfamiliar with your market and audience. In the end, if they've done their job right, you get back sales copy that spits back what you told them. All they do is plug your ideas into their swipe file.

The bottom line is, you get your stuff back. Somebody else will take your stuff, put it into their framework, give it back to you, and charge you a thousand bucks, five thousand, ten thousand, fifteen or twenty thousand dollars.

So that begs the question, when should you do it versus when should you not do it? When should you hire somebody to do it for you? My honest answer is you should be able to write your own sales copy, but you don't have to do it all the time. Typically, you're not going to do it when you don't have time.

And that's fair. That's fine. If you don't have time to do it, you're probably making money in your business, and it's worth it to you to be able to hire somebody to write the first draft. But you should be good enough at copywriting that you can look at what they send you, know if it's any good, and tweak it to make it even more effective for your target audience.

Give up the dream that you can hire a copywriter, tell them to write you a sales letter to sell your product, and a sales letter or video sales letter script magically appears a few days later that makes you money with no effort on your part. That is a pipe dream. It cannot happen. You'll do the work one way or another (and probably waste a TON of time and money paying for that lesson if you choose to ignore my advice).

If you choose to outsource it, here's how to do it well.

First, audition people with a small project. Do not hire somebody for ten or fifteen thousand bucks to write a 30-page sales letter unless you know them, know their results, or you have a good authority referral. I consider good authority God; everybody else is suspect. Do not make this costly mistake. Instead, hire three or four people to do a small project. Have them do something like write an email teaser. Have them write a set of headlines, do an introductory paragraph, or an offer summary. See if they can deliver something that makes sense in your market with your specific product.

The second thing is to ask for examples of their work. Read the samples and verify they were the ones who wrote them. Here's a dirty little secret about hiring copywriters: there are different levels of copywriters. When you hire somebody on the cheap, he's often outsourcing to a junior copywriter. The junior guy creates your stuff, but the person you hired charges you his fee while paying junior 30 percent of that. That happens all the time, not only with copywriting but also content creation. These people are all just whoring around with each other.

To make sure the work is theirs, get names of their past clients. Ask for these and talk to the people. "Hey, did so and so write this for you? How was the process? What were your results?"

Also, be careful that they aren't taking boilerplate sales copy and regurgitating you into the exact same thing they made for someone else in the same niche. I'm all for using swipe files, but not find and replace! One way to check is by using a plagiarism detector on Google. Paste in some of the copy and see if it shows up all over the web. If you see the same sales letter show up in five, ten, or fifteen different places with simple name changes, you know they use a boilerplate. You would be shocked at what people will do. Again, once they get your money, they're done. There's nothing you can do. So, be careful.

Third, keep in mind the size of the project you want them to do. Vetting somebody to write an email for you is very different than hiring somebody to write a long-form sales letter. The price will be different, too. You hire different people to do different things.

The biggest reason Russell Brunson and I created FunnelScripts.com was because once you understand that sales copy is nothing more than assembling a bunch of different parts through a process of asking and answering questions, and plugging those parts into proven blueprints and formulas, you never look at copy the same way again. You realize that's basically what most copywriters do. Not all, but most copywriters do that. So why not do it for yourself, especially when you have a cool tool like Funnel Scripts to help you do it?

When you get the copy back from the professional copywriter, you need to tweak that copy. You can't expect it to work right out of the box. They will hand you the first draft. You or somebody else will go through, work it over, tweak it, bend it, mold it, shape it, and test it to see if it's going to work. When you look at all the work you still have to do when you hire somebody, in most cases, it's just easier for you to do it yourself.

Summary:

- Hiring someone to write sales copy for you is not a set it and forget it affair.

- You should audition people with smaller jobs first to find people who can do work for you and weed out the ones who can't.

- Understand that you will still have to do work to get good sales copy back from any copywriter you hire.

- Understand that what you get back from a copywriter is only the first draft. You'll still need to tweak it, edit it, etc.

Secret #27
The Magic Desk

"The very first thing you must come to realize is that you must become a 'student of markets.' Not products. Not techniques. Not copywriting. Not how to buy space or whatever. Now, of course, all of these things are important and you must learn about them, but, the first and the most important thing you must learn is what people want to buy."

Gary Halbert

t's a challenge we all face. How do you get out of your head and into the mind of your prospects?

When you're writing copy or creating content, it's always easier to see how other people should be doing it, rather than it is for you to look at what you're doing in your businesses, or with your copy. In other words, it's much easier for you to spot the problems, or the successes, in other people's copy, or in their content than it is to detect the issues or the angles in your own. The reason is that you're too close to it. You can't get out of your head. You can't see the forest for the trees.

Let's walk through a cool exercise that helps you to get out of your head and into the mind of your prospects. This activity works best after you've researched your target market. You don't just yank this out of thin air. You have to know your target avatar Fred, that we covered in depth in Secret #8. Do this exercise after you fully define your customer avatar.

Here's how to do the "magic desk" exercise, which is guided visualization: read through it once to understand what to do. This technique helps you get inside the mind of your prospects so you know what they're thinking and more importantly, how to give them exactly what they want in a way they want it and explain it all in terms they can understand. As you do this, all I ask is that you have an open mind. It is going to seem a little strange, especially if you've never done a visualization exercise or practiced creative visualization or meditation.

This technique produces results because it allows you to find out what your prospect, your boss, your spouse, your customer, or your reader wants. Why is this ability critically important? Every person in the world has their mind tuned in to one radio station and one radio station only. Its call letters are WIIFM, which stands for, What's In It For Me. Your ability to tune in to other people's radio stations has a significant impact on your success or failure in life. No matter where you are in life, no matter how much money you make, no matter how happy or sad you are, no matter your goals, your hopes, your dreams, or your desires, no matter whether you want more money, more love, more peace, more happiness, or more satisfaction, you must be able to meet the needs of other people in a way they want so you can get what you want.

Satisfying other people's wants—emotional, financial, spiritual, or any other wants—the way they want them satisfied is how you get what you want. It's not the other way around. The bottom line is, to get what you want, you first have to know what other people want and give it to them (or sell it to them, as the case may be). If you're going to change the economic, social, or other circumstances of your life, other people play a big part in helping you achieve that.

The number one objective of doing this exercise is to raise your level of empathy with your customers or your prospects and tune in to their WIIFM, their What's In It For Me radio station. The word *empathy* gets misused most of the time you see or hear it. Webster's defines empathy as "A vicarious experience of the feelings, thoughts, or attitudes of another."

Some people call it being in tune with another person or in sync. Empathy means you feel and think about something the same way they feel and think. By learning how to get into this empathetic state quickly, you massively improve your ability to communicate with other people. Maybe you've noticed this in yourself. I know I have. When I'm around somebody that I have a high level of empathy for, I start talking like them, taking on their mannerisms, and in some cases, taking on their accent, speech patterns, and thought patterns. I noticed this about myself a long time ago, when I was in a college at the fraternity house. I saw myself doing it, but never understood why. I certainly didn't understand the power of using it to motivate others until much later.

Also, I have a background in the theater. Being able to empathize with the person or the character you're portraying is a big part of method acting. That's what we want. We want to play the role of a customer so well that we end up becoming the customer. Then the customer will tell us exactly what they want with the words, thoughts, and fears they have. We can then use this information to sell them. This technique is powerful. Be careful not to abuse it. You can and should learn to fully empathize with the customer, the prospect, or anyone else you want to motivate in some way. If you can get inside their minds, then you can feel their fear, and know what you have to offer them, so they feel more secure.

If you can get inside their mind and feel their pain, then you'll know the relief they want. If you can get inside their mind and feel their problems, then you can offer solutions that speak directly to their brain. One of the things many copywriters miss out on is the fact that, if you can identify a person's emotional greed, which they are afraid to admit, then you can offer them more of what they want.

This exercise will help you not only get in touch with what they want, but also to get in touch with their fears, their pain, their problems, and their innermost desires, so you can help them get what they want. Your ability to do that will skyrocket your ability to communicate with these people and motivate them to take the actions you want.

That's the background of this technique. What makes this technique even more effective is to do it after you've done a lot of research about your prospects or customers. You've looked at the websites they go to. You've read the magazines they read. You've watched the TV shows they watch. You've seen the keywords they use when they search the internet. You've done the intellectual research about your prospects, and you've got these ideas running around in your head, but you still can't connect with them on a gut level. The perfect time to do this exercise is after you've done that type of research. The more data you have about your target audience, the more useful this technique will be. Like anything, the more you practice it, the better you will get.

Before we get started, make sure the phone is off the hook, or the ringer's turned off. Make sure you have your cell phone on "do not disturb." Close your door. Make sure you're not going to be interrupted. Also, make sure you have an open and relaxed mind. Have a pen and paper or an audio recorder handy. I prefer a recorder, so I use my cell phone with a voice memo going while I'm practicing this. There will be things coming out of your stream of consciousness that you want to record without interrupting yourself to turn the recorder on and off.

The reason I prefer having a recorder is that once you enter the mind of your prospect, you'll be amazed at the stuff that comes out of you as you start revealing what that person wants. You want to be able to capture all of it because when you start rattling it off, it's going to come out of your subconscious quickly, and you don't want to miss it.

Write down specific questions to ask yourself ahead of time. It sounds weird, but it's just like an interview. You don't want to have to think about the questions you want to ask after you've entered the mind of your prospect. If you want to know what they're afraid of, excited about, what their problems are with something, then you want to have those questions written out ahead of time so they can serve as a guide.

It also helps if you write down your intention for the interview. For example, "My intention for conducting this session is to get in touch with my prospect's major problems and fears when it comes to writing their book."

Sit in a quiet place and close your eyes. Have the pen and paper or the recorder handy. Your specific questions are written out and readily available. Make sure you have enough space to write, or your phone battery is charged. Then I like to count backward from ten slowly. Now, with your eyes closed and your mind relaxed, feeling completely at ease and safe, visualize yourself sitting in a big, comfy chair behind a huge, ornate desk made out of teak or some other tropical, exotic wood.

Across the room from you is a door. The door opens and in walks somebody who turns out to be your ideal prospect. They look concerned. They have a problem they know you can solve, so they've come to consult with you because they know you understand their wants, needs, desires, and challenges. They take a seat across from you at the desk. In their angst, they speak rapidly. Though they're animated, you remain very calm and still.

As they're telling you about their problems, the stuff they want to solve, and the desires of their heart, suddenly their voice starts to fade. You realize you're getting up out of your chair, gliding around the desk, and you're still perfectly calm. Everything's cool. You get behind the person while they're still talking. As you move closer to them, you hear their voice in your ears and look out through their eyes. It's then you realize you stepped inside the mind of your prospect.

You listen to what they say, and you see yourself across the desk. You notice that you physically feel their fears. You feel their problems and their desires. It's this big, jumbled mass in the pit of your stomach. Then, from the other side of the desk, where you still sit, you ask them the questions on the paper. Because you've connected so entirely with the mind of your prospect, the answers flow out of you. You capture everything into your recorder or write it on the paper.

Some of the questions that lead to the kind of insight you're looking for are questions like:

- What terrifies you?

- What does that mean if that happens?

- If you weren't worried about anyone judging you, how would you describe that fear in words anyone could understand?

- What is your deepest desire for your life right now?

- What objectives do you have for your business, or in building a subscriber list, or in setting up your next funnel, or in trying to reach financial freedom?

- If I could provide that for you, what would you have to see, or what would I have to say to motivate you to have a burning desire for what I have to sell?

- What words would you use to describe what I'm selling or what I have to offer and how could I express that better in a way that would resonate with you?

- How badly do you want what I'm selling?

- How could I make you want what I'm selling more?

- What objections do you have to what I'm selling and what I can show you or tell you to overcome those objections?

- What would stop you from getting the results that I'm promising you can get?

- What could I do to sweeten the pot on my offer, my product, or my service, so you feel comfortable and eager to take advantage of it before I change my mind?

- As you look at my competitors, what have you seen that you like, that gets you excited, and that made you want to buy from them right now?

- What do I need to show you or prove to you that would turn you from a prospect into a customer who does business for me, or with me?

- What do you think is a fair price for what I have to sell?

- What else can you tell me that will make what I have to offer even more appealing to you?

- What other problems or concerns do you have that I may not be aware of or don't realize are important to you?

Once you've finished with the questions, it's time to draw the interview to a close. However, don't just open your eyes because that'll jar your mind.

You want to slowly pull back from your prospect and pull yourself out the back of them. You find yourself floating peacefully and slowly back around the desk and into yourself. Then you both sit there quietly, just looking at each other, knowing you've been sincere, open, and complete in your communication with each other.

Your prospect's whole demeanor has changed since they entered the room. They're calm, cheerful, and feel better because they know you've made a real effort to understand their problems, wants, and desires. Then, with a big smile on your face and theirs, they get up, walk out of the room, and shut the door.

With your eyes still shut, you start coming back feeling refreshed and at peace. You come back up, ten, nine, eight—feeling more awake—seven, six, five—feeling refreshed—four, three, two, one. Open your eyes.

Once you complete this exercise, you have some information and insight you can use. I've had times of revelations, like, "Oh my gosh! I've been looking at this completely the wrong way." Or, I've had situations where I had one tiny inflection, one word, one bit of pivot in the English that I was using to explain something that made a huge difference. But I've never done this exercise and not come away without some valuable insight to help me better understand and be more empathetic toward the people I'm trying to sell.

You can use this to understand how to meet their needs better. You can use this to help create sales copy that speaks directly to their wants and desires. You can modify your behavior when it comes to dealing with them in virtually any situation, especially on social media, where people can tend to piss you off. It's nice to be able to draw on some level of empathy which creates patience.

You can create a sale's talk, a webinar, a phone script, or any other type of interaction that's more in sync with what's going on in their head. Plus, you can massively increase your understanding of what the other person wants and sell it to them. If you do this, the insights you get as you practice it are worth so much money to you because you're able to get inside their mind, use the words they use, and give yourself the information to motivate them. The big thing to remember is not to think, "Man, this is weird," or "This is kind of stupid," or "This is kind of creepy." This technique is proven. Just use it. Don't get hung up on it.

Also, remember that the connection you can make with your customers all starts in your mind. For those of us who sell through the internet, this is going to sound woo-woo. But, if you think about it, you're transmitting thoughts from your mind through your screen and keyboard through the internet to their monitor and keyboard. Those thoughts are what get people to buy, sign up, and take action. It's all about having that connection, which starts in your mind. It's your mind. You can play whatever games you want. If you feel like this exercise is stodgy or weird, then it's stodgy and weird, and it won't work for you.

But if you're open, try to empathize and visualize through the eyes of your customer. You can use this exercise to craft headlines, to figure out bullets, to craft out a story, to write a sales letter, or whatever you're trying to do to suck people in and get them to take the action you desire. I use it all the time.

Like the old saying says, "Never judge a man until you walk a mile in his shoes." Now you can do more than walk a mile in his shoes; you can enter his mind and know what he's thinking.

Summary:

- Better copy comes from higher levels of empathy with your customers and prospects.

- Using a guided meditation like this helps you synthesize lots of information and data through the eyes of your prospects.

- If you think it's weird, it won't work. If you do it with an open mind, your results could be truly life altering.

Secret #28

The One And Only Purpose
of An Online Ad

*"The only purpose of an online ad is to get the right
people to click and the wrong people
to keep on scrolling."*
Jim Edwards

The only purpose of an online ad is to stop the right people in their tracks and get them to click. (I could stop this secret right here and, if you just took that last sentence to heart, you'd beat out 95% of your competitors). Anything else, such as branding or the other BS people spout, is entirely untrue. The only purpose of an online ad is to get the right people to stop and click. That's it.

You've seen those ads on Facebook or other sites. The courses that promise to teach you the magic formula for writing ads. They've got the ad that's going make you rich. You used to see TV infomercials that had the idea of little ads equal big profits. These ads promise to teach you to write the perfect ad to bring an avalanche of customers on social media, on Facebook, on LinkedIn, on Instagram, on Google AdWords, or even through direct mail. They play on your hidden desire (and belief) that if you could figure out that one perfect ad, you'd make a pile of cash.

These promises to deliver are enticing because you've probably failed more than you've succeeded in your past ads without their magic formula. Here's the thing. If you're honest, you secretly hate them for their success. How do you feel about those ads that make you feel stupid because they know how to create amazing ads and you don't? How do you feel when you see their pictures depicting their success?

Do you wonder if they're good at running ads for everything, or are they just good at running ads on Facebook for this high price course on how to run ads on Facebook? If that sounds like your experience then trust me, you're not alone. I've been there too. Let me share with you a few thoughts I've learned over the last 25 years of running ads online.

In this secret, there are five truths about ads. It's like five secrets within a secret. If that isn't over-delivering, I don't know what is.

The first truth about ads

Again, the only purpose of an online ad is to get the right people to click your link. I would rather have a hundred of the right people click my link than ten thousand people who aren't the right fit. That's how you waste money on ads.

If your ad targets the right kind of people, you pay a lot less money. You spend less money because fewer people click on your ad. If more of the right people click, your costs go down dramatically and quickly because you're not sending the wrong people through to your landing page.

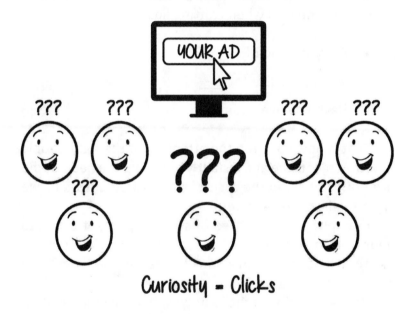

Curiosity = Clicks

The second truth about ads

Curiosity is key. It is the number one way you get the right people to click. If your ad makes someone curious, you'll get the click. That's it. Make them curious. The whole purpose of an ad is to get the right people to click. In our attention deficit, attention-starved world where people give you less time because they don't have time to pay attention, the number one thing that will get anybody to click your ad is curiosity.

What is it? How do they do that? Typically those are the two questions you want to create in the mind of your potential customers so they will click your ad.

The third truth about ads

If you don't know where to start when writing an ad, ask a question. That's all you have to do. Three basic questions serve me well when crafting ads.

- Are you tired of _____?

- Would you like to _____?

- Have you ever wanted to _____?

That is how you grab the attention of the right people in your target niche and instantly eliminate the people who are not. (Notice, in the case of these three questions we want to elicit a Yes answer.)

Examples: Are you tired of struggling to get traffic to your website? Would you like to write a book? Would you like to write and publish a book? Have you ever wanted to be an author?

Here's the thing. If they say "yes," you've grabbed their attention. Then you use curiosity to get them to click. If they say "no," they're not going to click your ad, so it doesn't cost you anything. Is that an awesome win-win bonus? Of course it is. Ask them if they're tired of being in pain or living in fear. Ask them if they'd like to get a powerful benefit or a cool payoff. Ask them if they've ever wanted to do something cool.

Asking a question is the best place to start when writing ads, especially if you've never written ads before. You can even use the question as your headline in your ad.

A little side note for you. One day, I saw a graphical ad on Facebook that blew my mind. It was a graphic with a one-line question in plain black text on a white background. No image. The text was the image. It grabbed my attention, so I clicked it. The person running the ad was a friend of mine. His picture was plastered all over the front of the landing page. I called him and asked, "Hey, dude, I saw your ad. How's that going?" It was offhand conversational, like guys do.

He told me he's slaying it. I've adapted this technique to my existing knowledge about using questions in my ads. In the past, I used pictures with text to ask the question, but up to that point, I had never made the text the image. Try it and see what kind of results you get.

The fourth truth about ads

AIDA is BS. What the heck is AIDA? AIDA was, and still is, the gold standard advice for offline print advertising. It's an acronym for

- Catch their Attention
- Stimulate their Interest
- Build their Desire
- Drive them to Action

You need to grab somebody's attention, usually with a headline. You could pique their interest with a picture. Then, you stir their interest and amplify their desire with a promise followed by an enticement to take action.

AIDA was a perfect formula to get someone up off their butt, in their car, and to your physical store. I am not saying that this doesn't work. But for online advertising, you don't need it. Remember that the whole purpose of an online ad is to get the right people to click on your ad. That's it.

You only need three steps. Step one is an attention grabber. You typically do this with a headline in a text ad, a picture in an image ad or a social media ad, or the first thing you do or show on the screen along with the first words out of your mouth in a video ad.

Think about Facebook. Think about Instagram. Think about Twitter. Think about LinkedIn. What makes you stop when you're scanning through those sites? It's not the headline. It's the picture. When watching a video, your decision to keep paying attention happens in the first few seconds. That's why Facebook measures the metrics of success for a video ad in three second views.

Therefore, what happens in the first three seconds of that video is the most critical part of that entire video. Whether people stick around or bail depends on what you say and show in the first three seconds. Use emotion to grab their attention. Talk about payoffs or penalties. Talk about outcomes or obstacles. Talk about the things they want or don't want. You want to go after emotion when you're grabbing attention. You can't be in the middle. You can't play it safe. You can't try to be relevant to everyone. You must force people to make a decision. You do that by showing emotionally charged imagery, by using emotionally charged statements and headlines. Emotion is key.

Step number two is to create curiosity. Show them a picture or text designed to make them ask, "What is this? How can they do that?"

Step number three is a call to action. Tell them to do one specific thing. Most of the time, online you'll say, "Click here to _____."

Let me give you some examples. Let's say your target audience is people who need help with financial planning. Their desire is financial peace of mind or to get higher returns on their money. What's their problem? Wading through the confusing financial jargon or getting ripped off by inept financial advisors.

Here's some example ad copy:

Want the 3 financial planning secrets every successful entrepreneur needs?

Free webinar helps you achieve total financial peace of mind and get high returns on your money without knowing all the confusing financial jargon. Register now.

There you go.

If they say yes to the question, they're thinking, "What is it?"

Get higher returns on your money without knowing all the confusing financial jargon or getting ripped off by inept financial advisors.

"That's me. I want higher returns on my money. Yeah, I want to see that."

Click here now. Don't hate yourself for getting ripped off by inept financial advisors.

"What? Oh my God. I hated that last guy we had!" or "I hate this guy that we have now. What are we going to do?"

Free webinar reveals how to get higher returns on your money without having to become a full-time investment manager yourself.

"Oh, damn. I would love to get higher returns on my money."

Three small business financial planning secrets every successful entrepreneur needs now. Click here now.

"I have a small business. What are the secrets?"

You can laugh at financial planning problems if you follow this simple plan. What is it? Click here now to find out.

"Oh, man, I have to click."

Whether they want to click or not, they have to click.

Here's another example. The target audience is coaches who want to market better to find more clients. They desire to get more coaching clients, to make more money, and to enjoy more freedom as a coach. What's their problem? They're losing money on marketing and wasting time on prospects who won't sign up for coaching.

Let's look at some example ad copy.

Five marketing secrets every coach needs.

Five _____ secrets every _____ needs.

Think about how you could apply these proven formulas to your business.

Five ways to stop wasting time on prospects who will never sign up for coaching. Click here now.

Is this emotionally charged? Yes. Does it focus on some problem they have? Absolutely.

Remember, the whole purpose of this ad is to get somebody to click.

How to get more coaching clients.

How to get more _____.

How could you say this another way?

Want to get more.

Want more.

Want more coaching clients?

Want a higher return on your investment?

Want <whatever it is>.

Five secrets to make more money and enjoy more freedom as a coach without wasting time on prospects who won't sign up. Click here now.

Boom.

Let's review the keys to a great ad that gets clicks from the right people.

1.   You use an emotional grabber.

2.   You make sure that you have a curiosity driver.

3.   Finally, there's a clear call to action.

The fifth truth about ads

It's a numbers game. Selling more and making more money online with ads is nothing more than a numbers game.

From my experience, it can take ten to fifty ad tests to find one that works well enough to be profitable. Most people stop before they find the one that works. They give up too soon.

"Oh, man, I ran every ad under the sun."

"How many different ads did you run?"

"I ran a bunch."

"Exactly how many campaigns did you run?"

"A couple."

"Okay, how many ads were within each of those campaigns?"

"Two."

They run two ads and decide ads don't work. People who do that are dumb. It is nothing more than a numbers game.

Running ads is like one of my favorite shows, Gold Rush, on the Discovery Channel. That show is an excellent metaphor for running online ads. The people on the show run millions of tons of dirt from areas they believe have gold. They've done tests, so they know there's gold in the ground. They run the soil through these machines to extract little bits of gold from each ton or "yard." It's just a giant sorting process.

The same is true with your online ads. It's a giant sorting process. These are the people you think are going to pay off for your business. These are the ads you think your prospects will respond to. Now you run the ads to those people and see what happens. If it works, keep doing it. If it doesn't work, then test somewhere else. If the test is promising, then run a bunch of dirt through your machine.

Most of the people selling courses on ads don't want to tell you it can take ten to fifty ad tests because they know that sounds like work. Nobody wants to buy work. The best thing you can do is burn through those ten to fifty ads as fast as you can. Then, eliminate the poopers, find the few that convert well, and scale those.

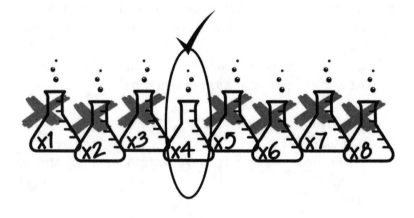

That's the magic formula. I just boiled down everybody's thousand dollar writing ads course to: write ten to fifty ads using emotion, curiosity, and drive to action, and run them. Get rid of the ones that don't work. Find the ones that do work and scale the crap out of those. The fact is nobody ever runs one ad that is an instant hit. That's not how it works. If you've tried to run ads in the past and failed, don't feel bad. Nobody knows which ads will work until they finish running all the ads that don't.

Oh, by the way, you never finish. It's a never-ending process. Your ad won't work forever. Think of it this way: you have ads coming; you have ads going; you have ads running right now. Think of it like a bucket brigade. You have ads you are testing, ads you are running, and ads on their way out the door. Don't get emotionally attached to that process. It's just how it works.

In the old days, could you successfully run a single ad in magazines and newspapers for years? Absolutely. Could you still do that today in print publications? Absolutely. Online, though, ads have a limited shelf life, especially on Facebook and other social media. Just because your ad is working doesn't mean you get to retire next Tuesday. You need to keep testing. You need to keep figuring out new angles and emotional hooks to use with your audience because it's never over.

Change your copywriting mindset to one where you want to "fail fast" with the losers and don't give up until you find the winners. To borrow a metaphor from the investing world, cut your losers and go long with your winners. Don't get emotionally attached to the process.

Summary:

- The only purpose of an online ad is to get the right people to click your ad.

- The majority of the time, you have to test a LOT of ads to find the few that work.

- Once you find ads that work, don't rest on your laurels. You still have to come up with more ads to replace the ones you're running that will eventually stop working.

- Grab attention. Build curiosity. Drive them to click . . . that's the magic formula for online ads.

Secret #29

You Can't Catch Fish Without A Hook

"Get the big point of your advertisement into your headline. Use your headline as a hook to reach out and catch the special group of people you are trying to interest."
John Caples

NO HOOK!

So, what's a hook? How do you create one? Where and how do you use a hook? A hook is an angle or a slant you use to create intense curiosity with your target audience. That's the key.

A hook's purpose is not to sell, convince, or convert. It is only used to induce curiosity. It pulls people into the rest of your sales copy.

Why do you want a good hook? You want to make your offer memorable. A hook pulls people into your world quickly because where the attention goes the rest will follow. If you capture their mind, the rest of them follows. Your hook catches a person's attention, causing them to want more information. Using curiosity grabs them and gets them to give you their undivided attention.

A hook is not a Unique Selling Proposition (USP). A Unique Selling Proposition, also seen as Unique Selling Point, is a factor that differentiates a product from its competitors. This differentiation could be the lowest cost, the highest quality, or the first-ever product of its kind. Think of a USP as what you have that competitors don't. But that is not a hook.

Now a USP can be significant to your success, especially when you're in a market with several competitors. A USP differentiates you as a business. A hook distinguishes your sales message from all others.

So a Unique Selling Proposition is what makes your product or service different from similar items. A hook is a lightning-fast story that creates curiosity about that difference. So here's an example. Here's the hook: "One-legged golfer outdrives Tiger Woods." The USP could be, "Our three-minute video fixes 90 percent of long drive problems."

Another example. Hook: "The story of a 76-year-old man who got me into the best shape of my life." Because it's an exercise product, the USP might be, "Special bodyweight exercise you won't see anywhere else but in this course." We capture their attention with the hook. But the USP differentiates the actual product from all of our competitors.

Hooks are often "hidden" stories or angles. It's important for you to look for these. When it comes to your story or product, the hook is sometimes difficult to identify because what other people think is cool, you take for granted. Look for the hidden story in your offer that would get people excited or at least curious.

Here are some hooks I've used through the years.

- "Rebel Real Estate Agent." Used to sell my book on how to sell your house yourself on fsbohelp.com.

- "Mortgage Loan Broker blows the whistle on industry corruption." I used this for a mortgage product based on my past life as a mortgage broker. The whole hook was blowing the whistle on people doing shady things. Which, by the way, some of the practices I detailed in my product ultimately were what brought about the financial crisis of 2008. That's not revisionist history; it is the truth. I blew the whistle on practices like charging extra fees or getting people loaded with variable rates they couldn't afford, ten years before it happened.

- "From dead broke with a heart condition and living in a trailer park with no heat and a leaky roof to internet millionaire." Now, that's a hook I've used which has produced mixed results, but it's got its place.

How do you create a hook? The process is as much art as it is science. I'll give you a quick overview, and then I'll show you a bunch of examples because that's where the art versus science comes in. A hook is often a one-sentence story about you, about someone else, even about a fictional character that's like your prospect. It can also be a combination of elements. Think of it this way: an unlikely character plus timing plus results. Or, a result without pain plus timing. So what do I mean by this? Let's talk about the one sentence story real fast.

"How I used a simple hack to go from bankrupt and living in a trailer park to become a successful real estate investor."

That's a hook I could use for a real estate investing course.

"Rookie realtor takes 52 listings first year in the business using this 15th century discovery."

You're probably thinking, "What in the heck is that?" That's the hook I could use to talk about the fact that every realtor needs to have a book. And what's the 15th-century discovery that this rookie realtor used? In 1440, Gutenberg invented the printing press. You might say, "Man, that's a stretch." That's a hell of a good stretch. It's finding the creative story to go with the hook. Any realtor will read that and say, "A rookie took 52 listings their first year using a 15th-century discovery? What is this? I need to read more." That's all we want.

Here's another:

"Ex-pizza delivery guy shows you a weird trick to become a bestselling author in a weekend."

I could use this hook because I delivered pizzas for Domino's for three years. So I'm an ex-pizza delivery guy. I can show you a trick to become a best-selling author on Amazon over a weekend. Absolutely can. Using social media, your friends, and timed buying, I can show you how to become a best-selling author actually in a day. But a weekend sounds cooler.

And here's one more:

"Meet Bob. Bob used a 1600-year-old secret to save his marriage, and we'll show you how."

What in the world could be the 1600-year-old secret to saving your marriage? You don't have to explain it in the hook, but you use the hook to pull them in.

You can also use a combination of elements using a formula. So let's look at an example of an unlikely character plus timing plus results.

"Former janitor goes from bankrupt to paid-off house in eighteen months with profits from his e-book business."

That is a hook I could use. I was a janitor at Giant Food during the summer of 1986. When I was in college, I was a janitor. I used to get up at four in the morning, ride my bike five miles, open up the grocery store, and sweep and mop an entire grocery store by myself before they opened at seven o'clock. And I did pay off my house with the profits from my e-book business. Granted, I was a janitor in 1986 and paid off my house in 2002. So I'm combining these different things. But it's an authentic hook to use. It will create an intense amount of curiosity.

Let's look at another one.

"Part-time chicken rancher loses 30-pounds in two months thanks to the unlikely combo of Oprah Winfrey and a former U.S. Navy Seal."

Now again, this hook is my story. Part-time chicken rancher? Yep, we have twelve chickens that I take care of every day. I did lose 30-pounds in the last two months. As of this writing, I am 30-pounds lighter than I was two months ago. But what's with Oprah Winfrey? Oprah Winfrey is a big supporter and business partner of Weight Watchers, and I used Weight Watchers to manage my diet and lose the weight. And then the former U.S. Navy Seal is Stew Smith, my friend who has been training me for the last five years.

Do you see the art in taking these elements and combining them into a hook? Your mind can't help but think, "Holy crap! What is that?" That's the only response. Your brain almost disconnects, so you stop any self-control and have to know what it is.

Let's look at another formula. Result plus timing minus pain.

"Lose all the weight you want in the next thirty days without diet or exercise."

What? That's what they're looking for! Or that's what they think they're looking for until they find out it's the methamphetamine diet.

"Create and publish your outrageously profitable book in just three hours without writing a single word."

That's a great hook as well and entirely possible to do. Where and how do you use a hook? Use it as your headline. You can use it in your sales copy. Use it at the beginning of your sales copy. You can use it in the first paragraph. Use it in your stories. You can use it in your ads and social media posts. Use it in your memes and infographics. You can use it anywhere you want to grab people's attention. That's the beautiful thing about a hook; use it anywhere and everywhere. Use it anywhere to grab people, pull them in, and move them on to the next step.

Summary:

- A hook is basically a one-sentence story you can use to grab attention and create intense curiosity at the same time.

- Hooks are as much art as they are science.

- You can use formulas to combine different elements to create effective hooks.

Secret #30

Create Your Own Swipe File

"Get yourself a collection of good ads and DM (direct mail) pieces and read them aloud and copy them in your own handwriting."
Gary Halbert

Whether you've heard of it or not, all copywriters worth their salt maintain something called a "swipe file". What is a swipe file? A swipe file is a collection of advertisements, postcards, direct mail, catalogs, posters, flyers and anything that has to do with selling somebody something. In the past, it was built around direct mail, brochures, or something you received in print.

But, why do you need one? When you sit down to write sales copy, most people can't flip a switch and instantly start writing sales copy. Just like when you work out, any good routine includes a warmup, something to get your blood going, something to get your muscles warmed up, something to get your juices flowing. You need to be in the proper mindset to write copy. A quick way to get into the mindset is to read good copy. Whether it's copy you've written that's worked well in the past, or swipe file copy of other people's sales copy, read some to get warmed up. If you need to write some headlines, a simple way to get those patterns flowing is to read some. Same goes for emails, offers, and entire sales letters.

How does it help you? Your mind warms up with patterns that you know work. You won't have stuff in your swipe file that didn't grab your attention, or you don't know for a fact is getting results.

Who should have a swipe file? Everybody. If you're reading this, you need a swipe file.

How do you keep it? Well, there are two ways. You can create a digital file folder or a print one.

You can quickly develop a digital swipe file, and I encourage you to do so. Capture screenshots of things you see that you like or save the entire webpage. I use a program called Snagit by TechSmith, who also makes Camtasia. Snagit allows me to capture everything from just a single image to an entire scrolling webpage. I save those in folders with sub-folders like ads, headlines, calls to action, stories, and bullets. When I want to get my warmup, I flip through these quickly and view them as graphics on my hard drive.

For a print file, I keep them in manila folders organized into emails, headlines, sale's letters, my stuff and other people's stuff. I've even bound some things with a comb binder. You don't have to do that. How do you use it? Use it as a mental tickler file every time you need to do something. If you need to write headlines, look at some headlines. If you need to write bullets, look at bullets. If you need to write a sales letter, look at the sales letters.

Funnel Scripts started out as my interactive swipe file with no intention to sell it. It was my little secret weapon I used to create content or to create sales copy for webinars, special offers, product launches, or emails. What used to take me two, three, four hours or even days to put together now took about fifteen or twenty minutes. It felt like cheating to use this software (and it still does).

When do you add to your swipe file? The answer is whenever you see something that grabs your attention! I remember seeing a video game magazine, on the front row in Books-A-Million in Williamsburg, Virginia. One of the bullets said, "The Grand Theft Auto Vice City secrets you're not supposed to know." My brain immediately replaced the Grand Theft Auto Vice City secrets with e-book marketing. I used the headline, "The E-Book Marketing Secrets You're Not Supposed To Know" to help launch a six-figure website. I still remember the picture on the cover. It was a cartoon of a woman eating a Tootsie Pop. It was a very provocative cover that grabbed my attention. Any time you see something, take a picture of it with your smartphone, email it to yourself, and add it to your digital swipe file. It's never been easier to create and maintain a swipe file than it is today.

Finally, when should you start a swipe file? The answer is "Right now!" Because if you don't have a swipe file, you put yourself at a severe disadvantage. Of course, you can use FunnelScripts.com, and I would highly encourage you to do that. However, having your own swipe file of everything from blog post titles, to intros, to entire paragraphs, to just about anything else where you're writing sales copy will help you shortcut the process and save a ton of time. That's the who, what, why, when, where, and how, of having your swipe file. If you don't have one, you need one. If you do have one, use it.

Summary:

- Swipe files get your sales copy juices warmed up and going, just like working out.

- A swipe file can contain anything you see that grabs your attention and works.

- Your swipe file does NOT have to be industry specific. I use inspiration from video game magazines all the time to apply to my business.

- If you don't have a swipe file, start one. If you do have a swipe file, use it!

Secret #31
Polish Your Sales Copy

"'Finish your first draft and then we'll talk,' he said. It took me a long time to realize how good the advice was. Even if you write it wrong, write and finish your first draft. Only then, when you have a flawed whole, do you know what you have to fix."
Dominick Dunne

Y ou want to make it shine, Baby. When it comes down to making money, people judge your copy. People judge you by the quality of the words you say. Do a grammar check. Do a spelling check, a punctuation check, and a formatting check. You want to make sure that, when someone's reading or watching or listening, you don't stick your foot in your mouth and sound like an idiot. And whether we like it or not, or agree with it or not, typos and grammatical errors, errors in what you say, errors in layout, funky line breaks, all cause people to judge you negatively.

If you don't take the time to proofread your sales message, what are you telling your audience about the quality of your product? If you're selling information, training, or coaching, people judge your level of professionalism by your grammar, spelling, punctuation, and formatting. It's true. Get over yourself and stop thinking it doesn't matter. It does.

Check how your copy looks or your video plays in every different web browser—Chrome, Firefox, Opera, Internet Explorer. You need to see how it looks and plays.

I first learned this lesson in 1996 when I started my web design business. A website and sales copy I created for a real estate broker looked perfect on my monitor. Excited to show it to him, I drove to his house, pulled it up on his computer monitor, and it looked like crap. It had a gray background, and all the pictures looked like crap because his monitor resolution was different. That's when it smacked me in the mouth, and I realized, "Oh my God. I almost lost this account, because I didn't check to see how it would look to everybody."

Since that day, I always check my copy on different browsers. Whenever I forget, it turns around and bites me on the ass. You need to check to see how it looks.

You also need to check on different operating systems, including PC, Mac, iPhone, iPad, Android, and Linux. Why? Because how the message looks, how the copy displays on somebody's device is not their fault. It's our fault. If it looks good, we can take the credit. If it looks bad, we take the blame. Check how it looks under every conceivable condition, so you don't sabotage your copy because it looks like crap.

The next thing you want to check is the secondary reading path. With text, this means you scan your copy and see if you can get the basic message. Read the headline, your sub-headlines, and the P.S., which is the secondary reading path for long-form sales copy or print sales copy. People scan; they don't read. Can you get the gist of your sales message from reading the headline, scanning any sub-headlines, scanning the bolded words, looking at the pictures, and reading the P.S.? If not, you have some work to do. You should be able to make a compelling case with your copy when people scan it on a secondary reading path.

VIDEO
SALES LETTER

Here's something I guarantee most people don't do. Watch your video sales letter with the sound turned off. Does it still work? Now I can hear the groans through the pages: "Oh my God. Why would anybody watch a video with the sound turned off?" All videos on Facebook start playing with the sound muted. You want to have subtitles for your videos. Rev.com will do those for you for a dollar a minute, which is well worth the investment. All your video sales letters from now on should have subtitles so when people watch your video with the sound turned off, they will get the message.

One more thing about auto-play videos. I mentioned in another secret that the internet has declared war on auto-play videos. Chrome has taken it to the next level, and I'm sure other browsers will as well. If your sound is turned on, Chrome will not auto-play your video. It will automatically pause it, even if it's set to auto-play.

Another reason you want to make sure your video sales letter will work with the sound turned off is that a lot of people will watch your video at work where they can't listen. They're sitting in their cubicle with no speakers and couldn't hear your video even if they wanted to!

Now, get a second pair of eyes on your copy, or a second pair of ears and eyes for your video sales letter. That second pair of eyes will catch the typos, the grammatical errors, the issues with playing the video, or the video not playing, or not behaving properly. Nothing beats somebody else using their computer to review your sales message and ferreting out any sort of technical issues.

There's a story about a copywriter who always gave his sales letters to his friends. His litmus test was if they didn't ask to buy whatever was in the sales letter, then he went back to the drawing board. The idea was that your sales copy has to be so good that you could hand your sales letter to somebody, and if they say, "Hey, great sales

letter," it means your sales letter sucks. The only accept-
able response is for them to read your sales letter and say,
"Ooh, where can I buy that?"

Now this story may be an urban myth to a degree. Unless
the people you give your copy to are in your target market,
there's really no reason for them to buy. So copying this
idea as your litmus test for good copy might not be wise.

On the flip side, if you have some customers you feel
comfortable asking to review your sales copy who then
ask, "Hey, this is cool, when are you coming out with this?"
that's a great sign. But unless that's the case, you probably
won't have people who proof your sales copy respond with:
"Where can I get one?"

Also, don't get caught up in the throw-it-against-the-
wall mentality. Because of the way everything works
online, speed is often valued more than thoughtfulness
or methodical-ness. Your language matters. Your grammar,
spelling, punctuation, and formatting matter too. Don't just
throw it against the wall and then say the people who are
not responding are stupid. They're not stupid. These are
the people you're trying to get to pay you money.

Finally, when it comes to polishing your copy, think
about the slippery slide test. When someone starts your
sales message, you want them to go through the whole thing
and end up splashing down into the money pool without
any problems. Read your copy from the standpoint of the
slippery slide. Is there anything in the copy, whether it's
visual, grammatical, the way that it reads, or the way that
it sounds, that causes friction? Your copy should feel like
a conversation with no funny breaks or jarring movement
from one thought to another. Does each section flow into
the next? When you get to the end of one section, have
you segued well into the next one? If not, smooth out the
language so it flows.

That's it. That's how you make your copy shine.

Summary:

- People judge your sales copy by the format, form, grammar, spelling, and punctuation as much as they do the content.

- Get a second pair of eyes on your copy to look for errors.

- Ensure your secondary reading path makes sense. People should be able to skim your sales copy and get the gist of your sales message in a compelling way.

- Watch your video sales letters with the sound turned off. Would you still buy?

Everything Else You Need To Know About Sales Copywriting

We covered some great stuff in those secrets. But before we finish, here are some additional questions I get asked every time I teach these copywriting secrets.

What makes copywriting different from regular writing?

It's your intention. What is your purpose when you're writing? Do you want to entertain? Are you trying to convey information only, or do you want people to take some specific action?

Copywriting leads someone to take a specific action. That action can be to click a link, to buy something, to fill out a form, to opt-in for something, to request a phone call, or to make a phone call. When you think about it from this standpoint a lot more things are copywriting than you realize.

Blog posts are copywriting.

Facebook posts are copywriting

Instagram posts are copywriting.

Even memes are copywriting if you use them certain ways.

If you create content and your intention is to get somebody to click a link, to go to a specific page, to request information, to fill out a form, to opt-in, to request a phone call, or to make a phone call, then all these things are copywriting.

So, I think it would be wise to expand your definition of what copywriting is, and look at what you're doing on a regular basis as copywriting, rather than just writing or creating content.

How much has the art/science of copywriting changed over the years?

That's an interesting question. I can only answer the question from the time I started to write the ads at the bank that made the compliance department rip their hair out up through today. That's a 25-year span.

A significant change is you don't get as much time with people today. It used to be that you could give more information and keep people's attention. Now, in the online world, you only have a few seconds to grab people's attention and hold their attention.

Secondly, curiosity seems to be a lot more important than it was. I think that's linked to the amount of time you do and don't have to get and keep people's attention. So you've got to be faster to stimulate people and pull them in. You also have to get to the point quicker.

As far as how is it the same? You are still solving people's problems, satisfying desires, showing them you can help them change their situation for the better. I don't think that's ever going to change. Go back and review Secret #3 for the top ten reasons why people buy. That was a game-changer for me in my copywriting career. Instead of talking in generalities, if I knew why people were going to want to buy, that made writing copy a lot easier because it gave me a focus, a filter, and a framework.

What, in your opinion, makes the copy so good they can't refuse to buy?

The short answer is your copy makes them believe they're going to get the result they want from what you're selling. So, if they believe that they're going to solve their problem, going to get their desire, going to make that money, save that money, save that time, avoid that effort, escape that pain, or whatever it is, they can't refuse to buy . . . if they believe.

It comes down to hooking them, to having an emotional appeal. It comes down to having the proof that you can deliver not only for yourself but also for them. That's the mental checklist that people run down. First, does this work? Second, has this worked for other people? Third, do I believe it will work for me?

Sometimes it can be as simple as a demo. The person sees how the product works and believes they could push the button that way or use the product that way. Other times, it's as complicated as having the proper case studies, using the right words, and having data to back you up.

But mainly it's the mental checklist people run down. "Do I believe it's possible to get this result?" "Have other people gotten the result?" "Do I believe that I can get the result?" So that's the short answer.

Should you write the copy before you make or create or manufacture the product or service?

I believe whenever possible, you should craft the perfect offer before you create whatever it is you're going to sell.

When you write copy for a product that already exists, your critical brain kicks in and says, "Does it do that?" Or, if you make a claim about something or give information, you think, "Well, yeah, I guess it does that, but am I stretching it?" These thoughts cause you to equivocate in your copy, which is a fancy way to say you tone down the promises in the copy because you're worried the product won't live up to the promise. So I'm a huge advocate of creating the ultimate offer, the best sales copy, and then developing the product that meets or, preferably, exceeds the promises made. The copy becomes the blueprint for the creation of the product rather than a spec sheet.

That's easy to do when you're talking about an information product or training because you nail everything in the sales copy, and then you make sure you teach everything you promised. With a physical product, it's still possible. You need to design the ultimate thing people want to buy, and then you manifest it as a physical product in the real world. Now, will you run into restrictions, especially with a physical product? Probably. But it's always easier to go back and say, "Okay, maybe we need to adjust this one little spot in the copy." or you say, "You know what? I'm committed to making this work no matter what, and we're going to find a way to make this happen. Let's modify the product until we can keep this promise!"

This is a wonderful strategy for creating copy that sells like crazy. If you create your offer, write your sales copy, your sales letter and your sales video before you create an information product, this is an easy process. You just create the ultimate offer and then fulfill it. It's the same thing with software. It's better to build the sales copy for a piece of software before you develop it because that forces you to make sure all the features you needed to sell it are in there. It gives you the strength and purpose when you inevitably run into a programmer who says, "It would be easier if we didn't have this. Is this feature essential?" If you have it as part of your public sales plan, you say, "Yes, this feature is necessary; let's get that done."

Do the same thing with a service. A service doesn't get delivered until after you've sold it. So make it sound amazing in your sales copy, and then deliver on the promise you've made to sell it.

How can I get good at copy fast?

The answer is the P word: "practice." The way to get good at something fast is you have to try. Then once you try, you have to be bad, and then you can be good, and then you can be great. The only way to be great is first to be good. The only way to be good is first to be bad. And the only way to be bad is first to try.

I suggest you write or create some copy every single day, but don't sit on it. Put some eyeballs on it and see what kind of a reaction you get. What do people think? What do people do? Or do people do nothing? The only way you will get better is to see whether people come across with money or opting in, or by clicking the link, or dialing the phone.

That's it. That's what you need to do. If you want to get good, you have to be bad. Before you can be bad, you have to try. That means putting stuff out there, trying to get people to take action, and then measuring and observing. Observe, "When I do this, this happens; when I tweak this, this happens." That's how you get better. It becomes an upward spiral.

How long did it take you to become an expert at copywriting?

I've been writing copy for over 25 years, but I am not an expert at copywriting. I consider myself to be good at selling. As soon as you consider yourself an expert, you stop asking questions. In the world of sales, you have to keep asking questions. You have to be able to say, "Wait. What's working right now? What's not working anymore?" You have to pay attention to what's going on. You must ask questions like, "I wonder what would happen if we tried this?" Those seem to be the questions that keep us moving down the trail, seeing what's working and what's stopped working, and trying a whole bunch of new things. Remember, trying leads to bad, which leads to good, which leads to great. Very seldom do you get to great, but good can get you paid too.

Also, operating from the standpoint of "How can I help people?" instead of "How can I sell people?" "How can I add value to the point people want to pay me? So they feel compelled to pay me? Or feel guilty if they don't pay me?" Those are great questions to ask.

Be very careful about considering yourself an expert at anything. It's much better to consider yourself a student of copywriting. How long does it take you to become an actual student of copywriting? The answer to that is the instant you decide to be one. That would be how I would reframe that question. You need to be careful about declaring yourself an expert at anything. The only thing I know I'm genuinely expert at is making mistakes. I'm friggin' good at that. For everything else, I try to be a good student.

How do you structure sales copy and headlines for a seriously boring commodity product with no obviously result-based opportunity, like credit card terminal paper rolls?

Now, this is pretty boring. I want you to think about the poor schlep who has to buy this commodity. The question that I ask is, "What's the emotion attached to it?" Thinking about credit card terminal paper rolls or something equally as dull, what are the feelings somebody has? What makes them unhappy or even super angry? What do they daydream about? What are their problems with this commodity that make whatever it is even worse?

This reminds me of a one-sided conversation I had with my homeowner's insurance agent. We met the guy once, signed all the paperwork, had three houses with him, four cars, a boat, a four-wheeler, a tractor, and an umbrella policy. It was a massive amount of insurance. I received a letter from the insurance company directly, not from him, that told me they were canceling the insurance on one of my investment houses.

I called him and asked, "Why are they doing this?" It was some stupid thing that could be easily corrected. I said to him, "Your job is to stay off my radar. I shouldn't have to think about what I'm doing with you. I should not have to worry about what the insurance is covering and whether it's working or not and whether you're going to give me any crap or not."

He said, "What do you mean?"

I said, "Your job is to stay off my radar. That's your job. I know that you're there if I need you, but you should not be causing me one iota of a problem."

I was a jerk about it, but it pissed me off that they sent me a letter telling me they were going to cancel the insurance on one of my houses, when I had been paying them $10,000 a year in premiums for over 15 years.

The reason I tell that story is because when it's something that's boring, perhaps the angle is, "We do what we need to do, we don't aggravate you, and we make it so you can move on with your life with one less thing to worry about." So perhaps the angle for this is to play up the fact that it's boring. Play with it. Say, "You know what? The last thing anybody wants to think about is buying paper for the credit card terminal until you've got a line of ten people waiting at the register, and you see the purple stripe show up on the credit card receipt. When you reach for a replacement roll, you find you don't have one. That's the time you don't want to think about credit card terminal paper rolls."

Also, bring up an emotional situation where they see that they should've paid attention to the credit card terminal paper roll issue. That could be worth exploring. You want to look for the emotion, for the story, for the case study, for the situation where it stops being a boring commodity product. Then show the prospect without the commodity, it's a major pain in the butt. Lead with that.

How do I find a better balance between this is about you and how awesome you'll be when you buy my thing, and my thing is really awesome and you should buy it?

The last thing you ever want to talk about is you and your product until you have talked about them and their problem, them and their future, them and their desires, hopes, and dreams. It starts with them. Whether it's the before/after/bridge, the problem-agitate-solve, or the benefit, benefit, benefit, then do this, whichever of those three techniques you use. It's all about them to begin with, then you transition into how your product, your service, your software, your information helps them get more of what they want or less of what they don't want, or both.

You lead with them. The story is about the customer. The sales copy is about them. That's how you do it. You don't start talking about your thing. You talk about them. It's like that Toby Keith song, "I like talking about you, you, you, you usually, but occasionally I wanna talk about me." Well, you should talk about them a whole lot more than you talk about yourself, especially at the beginning of your sales copy.

Does fear-based negative headline/copy content convert better than positive headline/copy content?

When you are talking about cold traffic, yes, a negative headline or fear-based headline, a headline that enters the conversation that's already going on inside of their head revolving around their problem or pain, will typically convert better. Why? Because it grabs and holds their attention. Remember, cold traffic is people who know they have a problem but have no idea if there's a solution out there. Also, they don't know about you or your product (yet).

When we're talking about warm traffic, these are people who are looking for a solution. They know there has to be a solution out there somewhere. So you can't lead with fear-based, because they're looking for a solution. You have to phrase your headline around the solution, so they know they've found what they are looking for.

With hot traffic, you not only phrase it around the solution, but also you phrase it around yourself and your product. They already know who you are and what you're offering. You're trying to get them to make that buying decision now.

Now, with the warm and the hot, you can then use a takeaway close, where you say something like, "Now, this isn't for everybody. We're only looking for specific people who want to _____." And they think, "Whoa. Wait a minute. what do you mean this isn't . . . ?"

This type of takeaway is popular now and referred to as FOMO—fear of missing out. However, you induce this fear of missing out, that's where you can use a negative later in your sales copy to get people to take action because they're afraid they will miss out.

How to take a client's boring offer and sexify the living poo out of it?

I like that. Sexify. The number one thing that sexifies an offer is emotion. You've heard this before, and it's absolutely true. People buy on emotion, and they justify on logic. So if you can amp up the passion, that amps up the buying power.

When I look at most people's sales copy, they talk about features. Sometimes they talk about benefits. But, rarely do they talk about meaning, which is where all the emotion is located.

Find the meaning and the emotion, and amp it up. Turn up the volume to either push them or pull them. The emotion creates motion.

I'm in addiction. Lots of pain and lots of shame/fear. How do I keep moving people to buying but not be overly pushy?

There are many different things you can do, but my suggestion is to use future pacing. Future pacing involves asking questions like, "What will your life be like if you don't stop drinking?" "What is your life going to be like if you don't stop taking drugs?" "What is going to be the impact on your kids if you keep doing this behavior?" "What's going to happen to your marriage in the next two, three, four, five, or six months?" "Will you even still be married?" "Will you be out on the street?" You don't have to be pushy to get the emotion amped up to the point where they're looking for any kind of help.

Another thing you can do is meet them where they are. "Hey, do you have a drinking problem? All right, well, lots of people do. Let's talk frankly for a minute. What's going to happen if _____? What if _____?" Then you move to, "Now, that's pretty bleak. Yep, that sucks. Now, I want to ask you something else. What would happen if we got this handled? What would your life be like if you did quit drinking? What would your life be like if you did stop taking drugs? What would your life be like if you stopped being abusive to your spouse?"

Paint that picture of raising them up and then here's the product, here's the offer, here's the solution. "The great news is you've already taken the first step, which is to realize you need to get some help. So, all you need to do is get started, and that is the hardest step. So, when you push that button, you can smile because you're on your way to recovery." Take them on that journey. If there's lots of shame, you have to shame them a little bit more. But then you help them get past the shame. If there's fear, you intensify the fear and then help them get past the fear. If the shame is bad enough, they will do something about it. If the fear is bad enough, they will do something about it. You have to make it worse and show them what the world is going to be like if they don't change. Once you've done that, then you throw out the life ring and say, "Hey, it doesn't have to be that way. I want you to see what life can be like in a very short time if we get this handled." That is how I would handle this type of situation.

How do I ensure my copy flows from step to step in the funnel and is consistent without being repetitive? How much of the same language should be used at each level?

This is interesting because this is a phenomenon I see all the time. People understand they need a landing page, some emails, a confirmation page, and a one-time offer page. They look at these different pages in their funnel and think that all the sales copy has to be different. However, you want to have a consistent message. You want to use the same words. The funny thing is, your emails can have the same language as your sales copy. The words on the page can be the same words that are in your video sales letter.

Don't reinvent the copy wheel. Use the same copy over and over. The more they see it, the more there's a level of familiarity and comfort that reinforces the message.

The other thing is to make sure that, as you transition from your confirmation or your one time offers, to your down sells, stylistically, everything looks the same. It's obvious the person is still on the same website. It's obvious it's still the same person talking to them. It's obvious this is still part of the same conversation.

It needs to look the same, read the same, and work the same all the way through your funnel, even beginning with your ads, emails, or however you're driving traffic. It should all be congruent, using the same words, similar pictures. Stylistically everything looks the same. Otherwise, you create confusion. And not just confusion, you cause uneasiness.

Any techniques or value in using local vernacular for copy? I recently was told my professional copy didn't fit the millennial audience.

When we talk about entering the conversation that's going on in their head, that means using the words they use because, otherwise, you're using the wrong words. So, this is good advice. You need to use the words your audience uses. It may be local vernacular, or it may be certain buzz words or keywords or phrases, so they know you are talking directly to them. You don't want them to feel like they're being talked down to, or on the flip side, like you're an idiot who doesn't understand what they're all about.

It's important that you use those words, but it's also crucial that you are genuine and don't overdo it. Targeting millennials, you shouldn't write like you're a 13-year-old kid, but you also shouldn't write like you're a 50-year-old out-of-touch adult. Sprinkle in the right buzzwords, the keywords, the phrases that will let people know you really do understand them. Rather than using slang terms or local vernacular, make sure you use the words they use to make it work.

Why do some words or phrases connect better with some people than others?

The answer is the words that connect the best are the words they use. If you're using words they don't use, don't understand, or don't identify with, then you're not going to connect at all.

Some other things you can do to connect better with people is to use verbs in your headlines. Why would you use verbs in your headlines? Verbs create mental pictures, which force people to imagine something.

Here's a quick example: "How to write and publish your own outrageously profitable e-book." "How to write" and "publish" causes you to visualize it. Now think about another headline. "How to be a published author." That's a little bit harder to visualize. This comes down to active versus passive writing. Search Google for active versus passive writing. Active writing uses active verbs; passive writing uses verbs such as is, am, was, were, and be. The *to be* verbs don't create motion inside people's heads. Instead, you come across as wordy and unclear. An active voice is clear, direct, and doesn't beat around the bush.

People get the message quickly. There are many courses available on active versus passive writing. Go check them out. I'm sure there are some free ones.

The other thing is to use copy connectors, which are transitions between blocks of copy. What do I mean? I used a copy connector there with the phrase *what do I mean*. Let me explain. That's another copy connector (let me explain). Use little phrases like that to connect various parts of your copy.

Another one is *for example*. For example . . . When you transition between the part of your copy where you introduce the solution with several bullets, then you might have a transition like, "At this point, you might wonder, who am I to make these claims about being able to help you with writing your book?" That's a copy connector. You would then show them, demonstrate, or tell them about yourself and your accomplishments. After you do that, you might use a copy connector like, "But don't just take my word for it, take a look at this." Or you might say "But I'm not the only one . . ." That connector introduces the testimonials or case studies section of your copy.

"Now, at this point, you might wonder how much this will cost?" That's where you introduce the price, do the price drop. Then you can say something like, "But before you make a decision, let me sweeten the pot even more," and you introduce your bonuses. Now you transition from the bonuses to your final call to action or the guarantee. Let's say you want to go to the guarantee. "Now, you're 100% covered with our money back guarantee." Then after the guarantee, you could say, "The choice is yours. It's time to get started." Then you go into the summary. At the end, you might use a connector like, "Oh, one more thing," to introduce everything at the end with a P.S., "Now it's time to choose."

If you think of this as one big conversation, which it is, this is a way to make your copy flow.

Several people tell me they don't read long Facebook posts. I wonder if it is because the posts are long or they don't connect to the long content together very well? It doesn't matter whether you're talking about long posts on Facebook, long articles, long sale videos, long webinars, or long sales letters. The people who are interested will read, watch, and listen. The people who are not interested will not. Target your people effectively, so the right people see your message.

If nobody reads your long posts or sales letters or watches or listens to your long video sales letters, then your target is wrong, or your sales copy sucks, and you need to shorten it. Don't get emotional about it. Change it. This is part of the getting good at sales copy. If it's not working, don't try harder to make it work by saying, "We need to run more ads." Maybe you need to change who sees it. If that doesn't work, then you need to say, "You know what? Let's try something different. Let's try something shorter. Let's try a different tack. Let's try a different headline. Let's try a different offer. Let's try a different call to action." Just try something different.

Avoid being a whiny little punk that says, "Well, this doesn't work. I must not be good at writing sales copy, and long copy doesn't work." No. *Your* long copy doesn't work. That's the difference. Own it. Try something else. See if you can get the result you want. So, if quite a few people tell you they don't read long posts on Facebook, that's great. Are they in your target audience? Have they bought something? Consider the source.

How do you use curiosity in your sales copy quickly, easily, and without pissing people off?

Don't use curiosity that is not related to your offer or your sales copy. The classic example is a headline "Sex" in giant letters. Then it says, "Okay, now that I've got your attention, let's talk about the world's greatest dishwashing detergent." Unless you're into some weird sex, dishwashing detergent has nothing to do with sex, and people end up pissed off.

Bait and switch uses curiosity in a way that pisses off people. So don't do it. Use curiosity to make people more "thirsty", more excited, and more interested in whatever you sell and whatever is in your sales message. A good example would be, "Could you write a book in three hours? Is that possible? Believe it or not, it's true and entirely possible. Let me show you how." That's curiosity-inducing and real.

Ask a question that seems beyond the realm of reality, but ask it in a *what if* way. "What if you could have the credibility of being a published author and only take three hours of total work to do it? Would that be cool or what? Well, believe it or not, it's true, and I can prove it." That will get some people interested in your sales copy. Lead with a question that has an outlandish, but supportable, claim.

As an aside, by asking it as a question, you can avoid trouble with the censors over at Facebook and Google because all you're doing is asking a question rather than making a claim.

Write what the target needs wrapped up in what they want, so it resonates. People buy what they want. Rarely do they buy what they need. Examples: "I want the latest Xbox game." "I want to lose weight, but I need to eat healthily." "I really want to eat a cheeseburger more than I want to lose weight." The problem is that people buy what they want. But the great thing is also that people buy what they want. You just sell them what they want and include what they need to get results (if they're willing to take action).

Whatever they want, sell it to them! But package what they want with what they need, so they get an authentic result. Just don't talk about the need much in your sales copy, because they don't care!

What can we do to keep people engaged and reading our copy?

- Use pictures that keep them moving along.

- Break up the text with bold bullets.

- Don't have big blobby paragraphs. Paragraphs should only be two, three, or four lines long max. Pretty much a sentence is a paragraph when I'm writing copy for the web.

- Keep it moving.

- Keep it about them, meaning it's focused on them, their story, their needs, their desires, and their problems.

- Phrase everything about yourself and your product as it benefits them, how it helps them, how it enriches them, how it will improve their lives, and how it will alleviate pain or dissipate fear. Just keep it about them, keep it moving, and don't drone on.

- Talk about meaning and focus on emotion.

Do you have a different approach or template when writing sales copy to promote a consulting service as opposed to promoting a digital product?

That's an interesting question because people always want to think, "My product's different. My market's different. My thing is different. Everything you're teaching would work for other stuff, but it won't work for me." The first thing to understand is that people are people, and people buy stuff. Whether you're selling B2B or B2C or whatever, it's a person that's buying. The person buys on emotion and justifies on logic. They want to satisfy desires and solve problems. They want to have some fun and avoid making mistakes.

If I were writing sales copy to promote a consulting service as opposed to a digital product, I would talk about how they will solve their problem or satisfy their desire by using the digital product. With the consulting service, I would talk about how they will fulfill their desire or solve their problem by hiring the consultant. It's no different. You explain how they get what they want. For the digital product, they get it by downloading this and clicking some buttons. For the consulting service, they get it by getting on the phone with you, and you solve their problems after a lengthy interaction.

There's no different approach. It's problem-agitate-solve or before/after/bridge. Where you are right now, which is the before. The after of hiring us or getting this digital product, and then positioning the consulting service or the digital product as the solution. You explain how they get the benefit. One is a service and one is a download.

Does the color of your copy on the page really matter?

The answer to that is yes and no. Yes, it matters that people can read it and absorb it, that it doesn't confuse them, it doesn't shock them, and it doesn't fatigue their eyes. Why do you think most books are black text on white or cream colored paper? Because that's the easiest to read. That's what we're used to.

On the flip side, you might hear things like, "Red headlines never work," or "Red headlines are the best." Be careful about prognostications like it's always this way or another.

You want your copy on your page neat and orderly with an easy-to-read color scheme that is pleasing to most people's eyes. That's it.

I don't know that the color of your copy matters so much to making sales, but the color of your text does matter if you want to lose sales. Do you want to piss people off? Have a navy blue page with canary yellow writing. I guarantee 99 times out of 100, it will kill your conversions.

What do you think about using a good microphone and dictation platform like Dragon Naturally Speaking to record the copy for version one and then edit?

Many people can tell their stories but freeze when it's time to write. In theory, Dragon Naturally Speaking and other software dictation platforms like that are a great idea. In practice, they're a complete and total pain in the ass (in my opinion). When you dictate using Dragon Naturally Speaking, you have to remember to say, end of the paragraph, new line, period, open parentheses, close parentheses, open quote, close quote, capitalize, new paragraph, all caps, scrap that, and so on. It's a total pain in the ass. What happens is you start talking but lose your train of thought.

If you want to dictate something, I suggest you use a service like Rev.com, where you truly dictate it. Then you send it to a human being who transcribes it. Rev.com charges $1 per minute. So, if it's 30-minutes, it's a $30 bill. There are other services out there like Dragon Naturally Speaking on steroids, where they work, but it's an automated thing, and they charge 50 cents a minute.

If I want to dictate something short (60 seconds or less), the best transcription option is to use my iPhone and record a note. For whatever reason, the iPhone does a better job of transcribing than any other software I've ever used. You can record little snippets this way.

If something is on the top of your mind, you need to capture it. I was on a Zoom meeting with somebody, talking about creating an email follow up sequence. I started to say, "You know, the email needs to say . . ." and I clicked the record button. In 58 seconds, I said what the email should say and turned off the recording. I sent the recording to Rev, they charged me a dollar and sent it back. All I did was format it.

I think Dragon Naturally Speaking sucks no matter how much you train it. Use your iPhone or use Rev.com or a live transcription service, and you'll be a lot happier.

Passive versus active voice.

Passive voice uses the words is, am, was, were, be, as opposed to active verbs. I encourage you to investigate it.

I help people beat their addiction, but is beat addiction a good enough hurdle, or should it be more direct like how to stop struggling with alcohol?

As with anything, when you talk about something like beat addiction, it's level one. That's the buzzword stuff people use. The problem is they're used to it. It lets them off the hook. "Yeah, I need to beat my addiction." So, now we take that down a level, and we say, "Stop struggling with alcohol." That's more specific and creates more emotion. But you want to take it to a level three or level four. Talk about destroying your family, your life in shambles, the financial wreckage, all your money's gone, you have no friends, your life sucks, and you're standing on the edge of a cliff.

Now the question becomes, will you jump, or will you turn around and do something about it?

Now, please understand that what I just said should not be used in any way, shape, or form. I'm not giving legal or counseling advice. For God's sake, don't ever tell anybody who's standing on a cliff they either have to jump or fix this, because that is a stupid thing to say. This is why I'm not in any form of counseling. Figuratively, that's what you have to do. You have to access those levels of emotion. As you tap into that emotion, using those emotionally charged words, you will get more sales . . . as opposed to keeping it at the top level where it doesn't hurt. In this case, you want it to hurt. You want pain because real pain spurs them to take action.

Can Funnel Scripts work without ClickFunnels™?

Yes. You can use Funnel Scripts to create copy for anything. You don't have to have ClickFunnels™, but we do recommend it.

Can Snagit capture a full webpage including scrolling down the page to get the entire sales page?

Yes, it can do that.

Could you please go into some more detail about copywriting for skimmers and alternative reading path?

When people skim, they read your main headline. They probably won't look at your video sales letter. They'll look at your bullets. They'll look at your sub-headlines. They'll probably read your offer with a picture of your product. They'll read the P.S. They'll look for the price. So this all has to have a logical flow to give the skimmer the gist of your entire offer.

Do you ever combine the before/after/bridge and the problem-agitate-solve together?

Sure you could, especially when talking about the before. The before can be problem-agitate. The after describes what life is like, which is future pacing. The bridge is your solve which explains the product.

How would I go about softening negative fear-based terminal outcomes of a violent attack, rape, and death regarding self-defense products and still have effective copy, as so many paid traffic sources are trying to step away from anything to do with violence or fear-based sales?

I don't know. The immediate thing that pops into my head is statistics because people can't argue with statistics. If you use US government statistics or something else related, maybe you can build around it and see if they'll let you do that.

Do you have a list of takeaways that you like?

The easiest takeaway to use is: "Now, this isn't for everybody. This is only for people who are _____." Then you fill in the blank. That's the type of takeaway you want to use. You say, "This is only for people who are seriously motivated to change their life. We can't do this forever, so we're putting a limit of 50 people on this." Whatever it is, that's how you do it. Don't over-complicate it or over-think it. Tell them you can't do this for everybody.

After you launch, what's a reasonable time frame to deliver the physical product to the customer? If you don't have it yet to ship, have that upfront in the sales copy for sure, but was wondering what's too long for delivery.

I wouldn't sell anything until I knew I would have it within a week or two. Preferably you want to have it in hand. So, just because you write the sales copy (but don't have the physical product in inventory yet), doesn't mean you run ads to the sales copy and take real orders. That can get you into problems.

Now, you can set it up to test if people will buy whatever you're selling. Set up your whole funnel, run ads and get people to the point where they click the buy button and think they are about to put in their credit card. But when they click that last button they see a message that says, "Hey, we're temporarily out of stock, but put in your email address and we'll put you on the priority notification list to contact you when we're in stock." That's how you can test whether it's working or not. Especially for a physical product, you don't want to take people's payment if you don't have the product ready to ship. There's too much that can go wrong.

Conclusion

I hope you enjoyed it!

My whole purpose in this book is to help you make sales. I have a damaging admission. This book is a sales book more than a copywriting book. It is about sales as much, or more, than copywriting because when you learn sales techniques, you can apply them to the written word and the spoken word. You learned how to structure sales messages and how to create a conversation that leads someone to want to take action.

You may be at the end of this book, but hopefully it is *your beginning*. I hope I inspired you to want to get better at selling. Becoming good at selling means getting good at making money. There's nothing wrong with helping people while making money. This book also talked about clear communication with your prospects. You definitely want these three skills (selling, making money, communicating clearly) to become part of who you are. It'll make a huge difference for you in virtually every area of your life.

Take the secrets in this book, apply them to your copywriting, and make more sales. Be authentic and help people make a difference in their lives in the process. That's a real win-win for everyone.

Finally, if you're like me and you love tools and shortcuts, be sure to check out FunnelScripts.com. This tool makes it push-button simple to create sales copy to sell virtually anything!

Copywriting Resources

New Tools!

Check out https://www.CopywritingSecrets.com/resources for a complete, up-to-date list of copywriting tools, tricks and resources to help you sell more . . . no matter what you sell!

Funnel Scripts

What if you could automatically write all your emails, sales letters, ads, video sales letters and more in a tenth of the time it takes everyone else? What if you could plug into the minds of some of the greatest copywriters of all time and use their secrets in an instant? Well, you can. It's called Funnel Scripts! Funnel Scripts is your ultimate automated, push-button swipe file for creating all the sales copy you need to succeed no matter what you sell! Get your free training and demo at https://FunnelScripts.com

ClickFunnels

ClickFunnels is the ultimate tool for putting your sales copy on the web to make sales, increase subscribers and build your business. No matter what you sell, ClickFunnels makes it super easy to get your sales copy online and start making money, without being held hostage by a tech guy or having to learn any complicated HTML. If you can copy and paste, drag and drop, you can use ClickFunnels to get up and running fast! Get a 2-week FREE Trial here: https://CopywritingSecrets.com/clickfunnels

Presto Content

What Funnel Scripts do for sales copywriting, Presto Content does for content creation. Do you need to write articles or blog posts to promote your business? Do you need to do Facebook Live or YouTube Videos? Do you need to teach classes, seminars, or create other content to sell in your business? Then Presto Content is exactly what you need! It's automated creativity at the push of a button. For a free demo check out https://PrestoContent.com

TheJimEdwardsMethod.com

Check out Jim's blog for updates, articles, videos and more. Stay up-to-date in the world of Jim Edwards. ☺

Snagit

Use Snagit from TechSmith to create your digital swipe files. Yes, there are other screen grab software packages you could use for free (Including Windows Snip & Sketch Tool), but for less than the cost of lunch for two, you can have the most powerful screen grab software in the world! Check out http://Snagit.com for more.

Jim's Recommended Reading

Seducing Strangers
by Josh Weltman

Scientific Advertising
by Claude Hopkins

Ogilvy On Advertising
by David Ogilvy

The Robert Collier Letter Book
by Robert Collier

Tested Advertising Methods
by John Caples

Breakthrough Advertising
by Eugene Schwartz

Advertising Secrets of the Written Word
by Joe Sugarman

Acknowledgments

I have to start by thanking my wife, Terri. For listening to my crazy ideas, managing our household and finances so expertly, and making sure we all have a stable environment that enables us to do what we do, thank you!

Thank you, Soosan Hall, my trusted right-hand for so many years now. Nothing I've done over the last 15 years would have been possible if you hadn't stood there in that tiny office that day so long ago and asked me "What time do you want me here tomorrow?"

Thanks to Dan Thomas and Dan Roam, the world's greatest mastermind partners, for encouraging me (rather forcefully) to write this book for many years. You guys have pushed me and helped me grow and I'm forever grateful.

To my "mortgage mom," Cheryl Morgan, thanks for kicking me out the door to make sales calls and learn by doing when I would have rather stayed in the office and messed around with charts and maps.

Thanks to all of the great folks at my very first sales job at Equitable Life Assurance Society. The late Joel Bernhard, Mike McNulty, Mike and Ken Mason and all the team. Though I failed miserably at selling insurance as a twenty-one-year-old, I learned one thing: great salespeople are the freest, highest paid people on earth.

A special shout out to Steve Powers, one of the finest examples of personal salesmanship I've ever met. Again, though I didn't set the world on fire when I worked with you and we haven't talked in twenty years, you taught me lessons about selling that have lasted a lifetime.

Thank you, Ray Roenker and Ray Bjorkman, for giving me my chance in the mortgage business where I had my first real taste of selling success at the ripe old age of twenty-three. If it hadn't been for you taking a chance on me, I wouldn't be where I am today.

Thank you, Andrew Lacey, one of the top real estate trainers in the country, for teaching me one of the most powerful sales lessons of my life: one good sales script delivered well can make you rich.

I want thank the team at Author Academy Elite, Kary, David, and Kirsten, for helping me pull this project together. Though I have already self-published dozens of books over the years, I needed extra help pulling this one together, and you all delivered. This would never have gotten done without your support and guidance. Thank you!

And finally, I'd like to thank everyone who ever bought (or didn't buy) anything from me: a house, life insurance policy, grave plot, weight loss plan, buying club membership, car, radio, cell phone, pizza, mortgage, e-book, software wizard, and more. Whether you bought or not, you helped me learn more about sales and the words that do and don't make people buy. For that, I am eternally grateful.

About the Author

Jim Edwards started his selling career very inauspiciously in the late 1980's after graduating with a degree in history from The College Of William and Mary. In his first 18 months out of school, he quit or got fired from seven different jobs, including selling: trunked radios, cell phones, insurance, weight loss, and grave plots. It wasn't until Jim landed in the mortgage business that he discovered the power of selling people what they want and being in the right place at the right time with the right sales message.

In 1997, Jim was one of the first people to sell an e-book online. This was when he got serious about learning the techniques of direct response copywriting (salesmanship in print). Because of his e-book sales, Jim appeared in the *New York Times*, *Entrepreneur Magazine*, and countless other online and offline publications around the globe.

In 1998, Jim also started writing "The Net Reporter," a syndicated newspaper column that ran for ten years.

Jim has gone on to use his copywriting skills to sell millions of dollars of his products, services, coaching, and software online. His real passion is helping non-sales people learn how to sell so they can share their message, products, and value with the world.

Jim lives in the tiny town of Port Haywood, VA, where he enjoys raising his chickens, playing with his grandkids, taking his wife fishing, taking naps with his dog, and going for long runs with a headlamp on dark, deserted country roads early in the morning.

funnel scripts

This is a FREE Training Web Class. There Are No Costs, But Seats Are Very Limited.

"How To Get ALL Of Your Sales Letters, Scripts And Webinars Slides Written (In Under 10 Minutes) WITHOUT Hiring An Expensive Copywriter!"

This Works Even If You HATE Writing And Never Want To Know ANYTHING About Copywriting!

REGISTER YOUR SEAT NOW!!!

https://FunnelScripts.com

Free Webinar Demo Will Show You The NEW 'Funnel Scripts' Software That Actually Writes Your Copy For You!